DOING
HOLY BUSINESS

*Dear Lord, we elect, but you confer authority. We occupy roles, but you form hearts. Help us to have the courage to lead by serving and putting aside the world's easier ways. Help us to emulate your apostles, not in the early days when they craved power and preference, but in the latter days after Calvary, when they prayed only for courage and wisdom. All this we ask in the Name of One who led by serving and suffering. Amen. ***

* Excerpted from "Prayers for the Year," by Tom Ehrich, *The Vestry Resource Guide: Now That You're on the Vestry*, 2004, published by the Episcopal Church Foundation in partnership with Forward Movement.

DOING
HOLY BUSINESS

The Best of
VESTRY PAPERS

Edited by
Lindsay Hardin Freeman

CHURCH PUBLISHING
an imprint of
Church Publishing Incorporated, New York

Library of Congress Cataloging-in-Publication Data

Doing holy business : the best of the Vestry papers / edited by Lindsay
Hardin Freeman.

    p. cm.

  ISBN 0-89869-515-5

  1. Episcopal Church – Government. 2. Church management. I. Freeman,
Lindsay Hardin. II. Vestry papers.

BX5950.D65 2006

262'.03 – dc22

                                   2006000468

Church Publishing Incorporated
445 Fifth Avenue
New York, NY 10016
www.churchpublishing.org

5 4 3 2 1

We dedicate this book
to all vestry members who give tirelessly
to make their congregations strong and holy,
their buildings hospitable and rugged,
and their hearts a place where Christ is loved.

Contents

FAMILIES

Foreword

Vestry Papers is in its tenth year of publication. This anniversary offers a benchmark for looking back over the past several years in order to bring you a compendium of articles representing the best practices in vestry leadership. The source for this collective insight is our readers, admirers, and leaders at every level of the Episcopal Church — local, diocesan, and national. The wisdom in this book, then, comes from those who are doing the work of leadership in the church. We hope you will find here encouragement for your ministry through new ideas and new ways of doing old things, as well as practical tips, spiritual nurture, and lifting the sights of your leadership to the larger perspective of God's mission.

There is really no other publication quite like *Vestry Papers*. In the great scheme of things, it is a modest venture. Yet for those who constitute our audience, it fills a need and a niche addressed by no other resource. Our editorial team and Advisory Committee make every effort to focus on the real-life concerns of those who lead Episcopal congregations. We and our writers are all engaged in active ministry, both lay and ordained. Some of us have led or are leading congregations now, and many *Vestry Papers* topics come from the current challenges we face.

After a decade, we believe that we have garnered much practical wisdom. We thought it would be helpful to the church to gather the best articles across a range of topics and put them between the covers of a book. Think of this book as a sort of reference guide. It will provide a valuable introduction to new vestry members and a refresher for continuing vestry people. Have you been given new responsibility on the vestry? Perhaps you will reach for this book and find answers to spur creative initiative and problem-solving solutions. Has the vestry task lost some of its excitement or challenge for you? When you peruse the articles here, perhaps you will find inspiration and refreshment. Finally, when your vestry term has ended, "and the busy world is hushed, and the fever of (parish leadership) is over, and our (vestry) work is done . . . " — to paraphrase John Henry Newman's elegant collect from the Book of Common Prayer (page 833) — you can pass on this book to a new vestry member who will be guided by your underlining and margin notes and turned-down page corners.

We care about our readers and continually try to honor their experience, and that extends to you, the audience for this book. We hope you find it helpful.

THE REVEREND L. ANN HALLISEY, D.MIN.
for the Episcopal Church Foundation

Acknowledgments

Glory to God, whose power, working in us, can do infinitely more than we can ask or imagine. — The Book of Common Prayer, page 102

This book is a product of many things: the faith of our readers, the expertise of our writers, an unshakeable commitment to learning and leadership development by the Episcopal Church Foundation (ECF). Without the Foundation's financial and programmatic support, neither this book nor *Vestry Papers* would exist. I am especially grateful to the Foundation's board of directors and its chair, Bernard J. Milano, and chair-elect, Dr. H. M. (Mac) McFarling, who have backed *Vestry Papers* without reservation.

Workers in the vineyard

Thank you especially to the nearly thirty thousand vestry members working in God's vineyard who read *Vestry Papers* regularly and provide us with enthusiastic and helpful feedback, and to the almost two hundred writers who have contributed over the years. All articles have been good, or else they wouldn't have been printed; it is only space that restrains us from printing all of them here.

In particular

I am grateful to William G. Andersen Jr., former president of the Foundation, with whom this project started, for his vision, faith, and enthusiasm. And I thank Donald Romanik, new ECF president, for his clear thinking, energy, and help in seeing this book through to completion.

Much appreciation goes to the Reverend Dr. L. Ann Hallisey, former ECF director of learning and leadership, who worked closely with me on *Vestry Papers* for four years. Her partnership, spirit, and high standards were key, as was her trust in the editorial and design teams to get things right. Thanks also to the Reverend Dr. William Sachs, the Foundation's vice president for learning and leadership, for his ideas, research, enthusiasm, and well of never-ending resources.

Marilyn Bond, *Vestry Papers* circulation assistant, gives tirelessly of her time and talent keeping our database complete and solid, builds strong relationships with subscribers, and managed much of the paperwork for this book. Former ECF research associate Susan Johnson was instrumental in developing Web interaction with *Vestry Papers* subscribers and doing key research.

Dick Kurth, Ward Richards, Dan Austin, and the Reverend Sarah Buxton-Smith, members of the *Vestry Papers* Advisory Committee, give freely of their ideas and help us monitor the pulse of the church. Kirk Hadaway and Bud Holland from the Episcopal Church Center and Steve Follos from the Church Insurance Group are endless sources of competent and current information.

I am particularly grateful to my ECF editorial associate Karen Greenfeld for her sixteen-year partnership on writing projects. Karen never puts a project down until it is as close to perfection as possible and has worked hundreds of early morning hours with me on *Vestry Papers*. Karen has the common sense to say, "Wait. Do you really want to say that? It might sound better this way...." Thank you also to Ira Berkowitz, owner of Monarch Communications, who has overseen design and production for *Vestry Papers* since its inception. He always gives us his full attention and best creative work, as does Kim Pawlowicz, our designer.

Special gratitude to Deacon Kenneth Arnold, publisher of Church Publishing. He is a delight to work with and his faith, confidence, expertise, and poetry will always be appreciated, as are the contributions of his colleagues, especially Amy Davis, John Eagleson, and Parul Parmar.

And thanks to the Episcopal Communicators, who have given *Vestry Papers* fifteen awards in the last three years, and whose professional standards and recognition are life-giving to writers and editors across the church.

Finally, my heartfelt appreciation and my love to the Reverend Leonard Freeman, my husband and soul mate, ghost editor and writer, business partner and friend. Without his contributions, *Vestry Papers* would be a much lesser product than it is today.

THE REVEREND LINDSAY HARDIN FREEMAN

Introduction

The work and play of vestries is a holy mystery — part spiritual exercise, part business plan, part community commitment. The range and diversity of things Episcopalians find themselves involved with when they accept service on a vestry almost defies description.

And that is why the Episcopal Church Foundation, in 1995, began a new publication for church leaders called *Vestry Papers*. One component of the impetus was the growing recognition and respect for the key role of laypersons in local congregational ministry, but another component came from the recognition of the growing complexity and diversity of the tasks involved as Episcopal congregational ministries moved into a variety of new models — corporate congregations, yoked ministry congregations, total ministry congregations, small and medium-sized congregations, you name it.

The oddity of doing business, and yet holy business, in an increasingly secular culture meant that most of us came to this service with little experience — and perhaps even some innate awkwardness — at putting business life and religious life in the same mix.

Garnered in the intervening years has been some practical wisdom about how we do this work, some best practices, some best avoids. Church growth always sounds like a good idea, but as Bill Tully recounts, he once truthfully told a new vestry: "We're going to grow, and you're not going to like it." Not everything apparent on the surface of things is as simple as it seems.

Hospitality needs to be a conscious decision, intentionally acted upon. Vestry roles and responsibilities need to get worked out within the realities of a particular time and place, because there is little detail in the canonical assignment, and the reality of a partnership between the clergy and the vestry is a different model than most of what we find in other venues.

Getting intentional about one's own spiritual life may be more than what some of us expected. And on the other hand, a common definition of spiritual — warm and fuzzy — may get significantly challenged in a place where the demons seem to show up almost as often as the angels. What we learn there flows over into how and what we bring to the task of forming the faith of others.

Of course there is all that money stuff: planned giving, pledging, stewardship, endowments, debt. Now "we've left off preaching and gone to meddlin'" when we talk to folks about their money. But there is a reason that Jesus' most cited topic, other than the Kingdom of God, was money. And it wasn't because it was popular. These things are always hard for everyone. But if vestries don't talk about them, who will?

And then, the building. A blessing and a bane for many, care and nurture of church properties is often one of the most important issues with which a vestry deals. We don't want to devolve into building worship (it can happen), but on the other hand, our buildings are often significant sacraments — outward and visible signs — of mission and the love of God for our communities and families.

Finally there are the conflicts and controversies that will arise along the way, and the crises for which most of us are not particularly prepared. There is some wisdom about how to deal with these too, thank God, and we offer it here for you.

So come along. We hope you enjoy, as well as gain some wisdom for doing this work to which Jesus has called you — the doing of holy business.

Contributors

Former executive director of the Episcopal Church Foundation **William G. Andersen Jr.** also served as senior warden of St. George's Church in Maplewood, New Jersey. Under his leadership, the Foundation grew into an international ministry and experienced an explosive growth in its planned giving services.

Deacon Kenneth Arnold is the publisher of Church Publishing Incorporated and has served most recently at Trinity Church, Morrisania, South Bronx. He is also the author of *On the Way: Vocation, Awareness and Fly Fishing* and *Night Fishing in Galilee: The Journey toward Spiritual Wisdom.*

The Reverend Dr. Jerome Berryman is director of the Center for the Theology of Childhood in Houston. The author of the Montessori-based Godly Play curriculum, he is also the author of numerous articles and books.

A prolific writer, priest, and teacher based in North Carolina, **the Reverend Tom Ehrich** is the author of "On a Journey," a series of daily meditations now received by Christians around the world. He is also the author of several books and a syndicated newspaper column.

The Right Reverend Thomas C. Ely, bishop of Vermont, has a long history of working with youth and young people as bishop, parish priest, missioner, and director of youth ministry programs. He credits many adults at his home parish of Grace Episcopal Church in Norwalk, Connecticut, for playing an important role in his formation.

A three-time senior warden at St. Paul's in Indianapolis, **Scott Evenbeck** is the dean of University College at Indiana University–Purdue University Indianapolis (IUPUI) and was the first lay president of the Consortium of Endowed Episcopal Parishes. A longstanding deputy to General Convention, he chaired the House of Deputies Committee on Education in 2000 and 2003. He is a member of the Joint Nominating Committee for the Presiding Bishop.

The Reverend Caroline Fairless is founding director of Children at Worship — Congregations in Bloom. Her publications include *Children at Worship — Congregations in Bloom; New Voices/Ancient Words: Dramatic Adaptations of Scripture; Hambone, Confessions of a Fake Priest;* and *The Bloom Box.* She currently serves St. James Episcopal Church in Bowie, Maryland.

A resident of Skippack, Pennsylvania, **Steve Follos** is a vice president of the Church Insurance Agency Corporation, which is overseen by the Church Pension Group. Church Insurance insures approximately 75 percent of Episcopal parishes and 82 percent of Episcopal dioceses.

Formerly the head of communications at Trinity Wall Street, New York, and the Washington National Cathedral, **the Reverend Leonard Freeman** is rector of St. Martin's-by-the-Lake in Minnetonka Beach, Minnesota. An award-winning writer, editor, and film critic, he is a *Forward Day by Day* author and regular contributor to *Episcopal Life.* His national video productions include *Jüurgen Moltmann: The Theology of Hope* and *Hildegaard of Bingen.*

The Reverend Lindsay Hardin Freeman is the editor of *Vestry Papers* and a parish priest at St. Martin's-by-the-Lake in Minnetonka Beach, Minnesota. She has served parishes in Boston and Philadelphia and has won numerous national awards for excellence in religious journalism.

The former director of diocesan programs for Giving Services at the Episcopal Church Foundation, **the Venerable Charles Gearing** is also a deacon at St. Bartholomew's in Atlanta and archdeacon for the Diocese of Atlanta. He takes particular delight in working with parishes and seeing their planned giving programs succeed.

The Reverend Canon Elizabeth R. Geitz is the canon for ministry development and deployment in the Diocese of New Jersey. She is an award-winning writer and author of numerous books, including *Fireweed Evangelism: Christian Hospitality in a Multi-Faith World, Gender and the Nicene Creed,* and *Soul Satisfaction.* She is also an editor of *Women's Uncommon Prayers.*

Bill George is currently professor of management practice at Harvard Business School and the former chairman and CEO of Medtronic, Inc. The author of *Authentic Leadership: Rediscovering the Secrets to Creating Lasting Value,* he sees his current calling as developing the next generation of authentic leaders through mentoring, teaching, and writing. George also serves on the board of directors of Novartis, Goldman Sachs, and ExxonMobil and chairs the board of the Global Center for Leadership and Business Ethics.

The Reverend Julie Graham spent eight years as coordinator of youth and young adult ministries for the Diocese of California. After fifteen years as a youth minister working in parishes and developing the Youth Ministry Academy with Church Divinity School of the Pacific (CDSP), she is currently working as a full-time mother at home with her three-year-old, teaching him the wonders of a loving God.

The Reverend Linda Grenz, an Episcopal priest, is publisher and CEO of LeaderResources, an Episcopal publishing and consulting organization.

The missioner for Latino/Hispanic ministries at the Episcopal Church Center, **the Reverend Anthony Guillén** formerly served as rector of All Saints, Oxnard, California. During his thirteen years as rector, attendance doubled and All Saints became a vibrant bilingual/bicultural congregation. He has also served on the Executive Council, the Standing Commission on Liturgy and Music, and the 20/20 Strategy Team.

The Episcopal chaplain at Cornell University, **the Reverend Suzanne Guthrie** is the author of *Praying the Hours* and *Grace's Window*. She leads programs and retreats throughout the United States and is currently editing a book of hours and devotions for children.

The Reverend L. Ann Hallisey, D.Min., is the national coordinator for Fresh Start, a diocesan-led program for clergy and congregations in the transition occasioned by a new call. In her tenure as director of Learning and Leadership (formerly Cornerstone) for the Episcopal Church Foundation, Ann developed programs and publications that continue to strengthen local congregations for mission and ministry. She is also a licensed marriage and family therapist and an experienced spiritual director.

The Reverend Ben Helmer is a recently retired member of the Congregational Development Unit at the Episcopal Church Center in New York. He continues to work with congregations and clergy focusing on vitality and growth in small congregations.

The Reverend Judith Hoover is the retired rector of St. Edward the Confessor Episcopal Church in Orono, Minnesota. With her support and widespread determination in the congregation, a new church graces the spot where the old one stood. She continues to do supply and consulting work.

The Right Reverend Katharine Jefferts Schori is bishop of Nevada. Before ordination she served on vestries as junior warden and senior warden and in a variety of diocesan offices.

Bishop of Louisiana since 1998, **the Right Reverend Charles E. Jenkins** and the fifty-four parishes of his diocese are raising $7–$9 million to build a youth conference center, provide seed money for three new congregations, and expand campus ministry. Bishop Jenkins adds this personal note in October of 2005: "It is difficult to describe the emotions I have experienced over these last few weeks following hurricanes Katrina and Rita. As my staff and I, assisted by the many talented leaders from across the Episcopal Church, work to organize our relief efforts to the people of Louisiana, we live in joyous expectation of the renewal that will come after this trying time in Christ's church in Louisiana. Please continue to pray for us."

Lisa Kimball is a Ph.D. candidate and instructor at the University of Minnesota. She was the 2002 and 2005 Episcopal Youth Event (EYE) coordinator and regularly works with congregations and dioceses to invigorate ministries focused on youth and young adults.

The canon for Christian formation at the Cathedral Church of the Nativity in Bethlehem, Pennsylvania, **the Reverend Anne E. Kitch** is the author of *The Anglican Family Prayer Book; Bless This Way; One Little Church Mouse;* and *Bless This Day: Toddler Prayers,* all from Morehouse Publishing.

The Very Reverend James A. Kowalski has been dean of the Cathedral Church of St. John the Divine since March 2002, and served as rector in Darien and Hartford, Connecticut, before that. He is also a Fellow of the American Leadership Forum and the Aspen Institute.

A former warden at St. Luke's Parish in Darien, Connecticut, **Dick Kurth** is principal of Richard Kurth Associates, a leadership development firm, and founder of the Power Polyclinic–Experiments in Living. He lives in Raleigh, North Carolina, and New York City.

The Reverend Eliza Linley is a priest, architect, and liturgical artist in Berkeley, California. She is chair of the Architecture Commission of the Diocese of California and serves on the board of the Church Divinity School of the Pacific and the Center for Arts, Religion, and Education at the Graduate Theological Union.

Caleb Loring III is a member of Christ Church Episcopal of Hamilton, Massachusetts, a trustee of Gordon-Conwell Theological Seminary, and principal of Essex Street Associates in Boston. He has served as a board member of the Episcopal Church Foundation.

The founder of the Episcopal Ad Project, **the Reverend Dr. George Martin** is a trained interim serving St. Bartholomew's Church in Poway, California. He is the author of four books, including *Advertising the Local*

Church. His ministry includes seminars and consultations in the areas of evangelism and leadership.

The author of numerous articles and books, **the Reverend Loren Mead** served from 1974 to 1994 as founding president of the Alban Institute in Washington, D.C.

An attorney and member of All Saints in Homewood, Alabama, **Bill Nolan** is the Episcopal Church Foundation's regional gift planning manager for the Southeastern states, comprising Province IV of the Episcopal Church. He works closely with vestries and individual Episcopalians, assisting them in understanding charitable estate planning and implementing their own planned giving ministries.

In 1995, the Episcopal Church Foundation embraced a new ministry of religious philanthropy and hired **Fred Osborn** to direct it. He retired from that position in 2005, after having built an explosive program in Planned Giving Services for parishes and dioceses throughout the country.

The Right Reverend Henry Nutt Parsley Jr. is bishop of Alabama and chairs the Theology Committee for the House of Bishops. He also serves as the chancellor of the University of the South, Sewanee.

In 1995, **the Right Reverend Claude E. Payne** was elected bishop of Texas at age sixty-three and cast a missionary vision for the diocese. In the nine years prior to his mandatory retirement, the diocesan culture was transformed, reaching out to all sorts and conditions of unchurched people. Outreach, finances, and attendance soared. Bishop Payne is also the author of *Reclaiming the Great Commission.*

A former vestry member, **Sharon Ely Pearson** is children's ministries and Christian education coordinator for the Diocese of Connecticut. She is a certified Godly Play teacher and Education for Ministry mentor and holds a master's degree in Christian education from Virginia Theological Seminary. She also represents the dioceses of Province I on the Episcopal Council for Christian Education (ECCE).

A former vestry member of St. Martin's-in-the-Fields in Philadelphia, **Sarah Peveler** is the director of training of the Philadelphia-based Partners for Sacred Places, a national nonprofit, nonsectarian organization promoting the stewardship of older and historic religious properties.

Sub-dean and vice president for academic affairs at the General Theological Seminary in New York City, where he is also professor of mission and world Christianity, **the Reverend Titus Presler, Th.D.,** served congregations full-time for nineteen years and has mission experience in Africa and Asia.

A native of England and a member of Trinity Episcopal Church in Princeton, New Jersey, **Annabelle Radcliffe-Trenner** is a founding principal of Historic Building Architects, LLC, in Trenton, New Jersey. Named "Young Architect of the Year" in 2002, she is committed to helping those who care for buildings in the public realm, including historic churches.

Ward Richards is a professional mediator and arbitrator. His ministry includes helping individuals and organizations, including Episcopal communities, productively address and resolve conflict. An active member of the Diocese of Georgia and St. Peter's, Savannah, he is on the Episcopal Church Foundation Board of Trustees and its Executive Committee, and he co-chairs its Learning and Leadership Committee.

The Reverend Dr. William L. Sachs is vice president for learning and leadership for the Episcopal Church Foundation. His next book, *Homosexuality and the Crisis of the Anglican Communion,* is to be published by Cambridge University Press in 2007.

After twenty-one years as a rector in northern New Jersey, **the Reverend A. Wayne Schwab** became the first full-time evangelism officer at the Episcopal Church Center. Still working in mission and evangelism, he lives in upstate New York and is the author of *When the Members Are the Missionaries: An Extraordinary Calling for Ordinary People,* published by Member Mission Press.

The co-editor of *A Failure of Nerve: Leadership in the Age of the Quick Fix,* by Edwin H. Friedman, family psychotherapist **Margaret M. "Peggy" Treadwell,** M.S.W., L.I.C.S.W., is the director of the Counseling Center at St. Columba's in Washington, D.C. She has been active in education and counseling for thirty years.

The Reverend William McD. Tully has been rector of St. Bartholomew's Church in New York City since 1994. When he arrived, attendance for Sunday morning services averaged around two hundred; now it is eleven hundred. In 2001, St. Bart's was selected as one of three hundred excellent congregations in a nationwide Lilly-funded survey, the only such Episcopal congregation in New York State.

The Reverend Dr. Malcolm C. Young is rector of Christ Episcopal Church in Los Altos, California. In September 2004, he received his doctoral degree in theology from Harvard University, where he wrote a dissertation on Henry David Thoreau.

DOING
HOLY BUSINESS

ONE

Church Growth

Follow me and I will make you fish for people. — Matthew 1:19

Go therefore and make disciples of all nations, baptizing them in the name of the Father and the Son and the Holy Spirit. — Matthew 28:19

Perhaps it's ironic that this book starts with a chapter on church growth. After all, lots of other things are normally on the front burners for vestries: financial stability, church attendance, pledging, buildings and grounds.

Truth be told, we're taking our clue here from Jesus. Like bookends, his words and actions inviting others into the Christian life opened and closed his earthly ministry. So we figure there can't be a better starting point.

Granted, such reaching out doesn't always come easily. Discussing leaky roofs is probably a little easier than inviting others to join and being prepared for change when they do.

No doubt the disciples felt uncomfortable, too — but at Jesus' urging, they jumped right in. And jumping in is what Christians, and especially vestry members, are asked to do time and time again — whether it is taking leadership in a pledge campaign, dishing up food in a soup kitchen, or praying for the health of your congregation.

So, much like the early disciples, just get started. Keep the big picture in mind. And as our first writer, Bishop Claude Payne points out, if there are stumbling blocks in your congregation that preclude growth, take steps to fix them.

Have courage. Have fun. And most of all, have faith.

First There Must Be Health

CLAUDE E. PAYNE

Health has always been the ingredient of a vibrant church. If a church at any level — local, regional, national, or global — is healthy, with robust self-esteem, trusting relationships, respected leadership, and life-affirming goals, it will radiate confidence and hope.

Yet so often in the church, good health is assumed. Lofty goals are set without any consideration of an internal audit. This can lead to disappointment and frustration.

So the first huge, often daunting, fundamental task for any church embarking on an evangelism initiative is internal scrutiny. What is the existing church culture? Are there trusting relationships, healthy self-esteem, respected leadership, and life-affirming goals?

Usually, the evaluation of leadership is the most difficult. Few want to critique a rector or a vicar. Certainly not a bishop. But a fact of communal existence is that a group, whatever the size, will never develop beyond the vision and competence of its leader.

Evangelism necessitates a completely reordered and dynamic church culture whose goal goes far beyond survival to full-blown mission.

This doesn't mean that those clergy who do not possess the personal gifts for congregational leadership are not competent. They often have tremendous skills for pastoral work. So they need to be in positions where they can utilize those skills. When that happens both they and the places they serve can thrive. And health will reign.

The laity also need evaluation. If there are not healthy relationships, high levels of trust, and a ready willingness among lay leaders, those issues have to be addressed before going any farther. Health demands it.

Transformation by divine power

For evangelism to flourish, the clergy leader must place high value on "proclaiming by word and example the good news of God in Christ," as the baptismal covenant states. So a leader must be driven by the exciting possibility that the lives of those possessing no faith community will be transformed by divine power through efforts of the faithful.

Let me embellish with a story. Early in my episcopate I visited a congregation — we called them missionary outposts to reinforce the diocesan vision — which was in a small town where there was little growth. The lack of young people was a major concern.

They had an energetic vicar with leadership skills who believed firmly in the evangelism imperative. The congregation was composed mostly of retired people. When I asked whether there were other retired people around, they said yes. So I suggested that they missionize the retired folk and not be paralyzed by their lack of younger people.

They were already in a splendid posture for evangelism. They had a resale shop as an outreach ministry. This established their integrity as a church that cares for those beyond it.

Several years later I found they had not only attracted retirees but also had several younger folk in the congregation, including children. Their culture had changed from a focus on survival and a preoccupation with the young people they didn't have to one of miraculous possibility. This brought new life first to them, and that life became an attraction to others. Another thrilling thing for me was that it proved again that small churches can grow.

Not maintaining, but building

Creating an engaging, open, and loving aggressive church culture is a prerequisite for health. It is tough. People have to be convinced that Christians are called not simply to maintain the church, but to build it through discipleship. Clergy leadership must be prepared to preach, teach, and live this vision, realizing that change comes slowly, one person at a time. Lay leadership has to be developed and nurtured in the Anglican way of evangelism.

Evangelism can also serve to transcend some of the dysfunction in the Episcopal Church around controversial issues. These issues won't be settled soon. Thus the timely opportunity is to concentrate on what can be done and done well. Furthermore, if those of differing opinions on vital issues can find an exciting mission centered on evangelism rather than fighting each other, they can provide a model of health for society and find that seekers of a greater diversity will be attracted to it.

It is immeasurably helpful if the diocese is healthy to the extent that it can support the local church with both a godly vision for mission and programmatic resources. Dioceses electing bishops would also be well served by choosing nominees with creative leadership skills and a passion for evangelism.

Money follows mission

Finally, remember that money always follows mission. People are by far the greatest asset of the church. They always have been. The earliest disciples were poor. Yet in the richness of their faith and their dedication to

Jesus' vision of a Kingdom of God now, their reliance upon the promised Holy Spirit led them into a miraculous expectation that led from victory to victory.

So to the faithful the harvest is always plenteous. But evangelism is not a new program. It necessitates a completely reordered and dynamic church culture whose goal goes far beyond survival to full-blown mission. This is true health.

Grow or Go:
A Radical One-Point Program
WILLIAM McD. TULLY

My first talk to St. Bart's, after my inaugural sermon, came at the first of a series of meetings to share my thinking and hear from my new parishioners. I remember it as if it were yesterday.

There was some urgency in the air. People knew that the parish profile and the terms of my call had made clear that the parish was living on borrowed time and inherited money. It was agreed that at the present rate, we had about three years before closing—or at least until ceasing to be a church rather than a landmark museum.

I asked that someone get a pen and paper and take dictation. Just one sentence, and I'll never dictate again. A few nervous laughs. A couple of looks that masked the thought, *Yeah, right. What do rectors ever do but dictate?*

I said simply, "We will grow, and you won't like it." Then I asked that someone save the paper. I was fairly sure I'd want to refer to it again.

Before I could get far into the talk, several hands were impatiently raised. "No, no, that's why we called you. We want to grow. We have to grow."

Preach the Gospel everywhere you go — and if you must, use words.   —St. Augustine

---

Agreed, I said. We want to, we have to, and we will. But you won't like what you'll have to get used to. There will be much change, and new people with new ideas and new needs. You'll wonder who they are. You'll wonder even more why such a fuss is being made over those who haven't given what you've given and lived through what you've lived through. You'd be less than human if you didn't feel that way, I said. I meant it, and I had experience to back it up.

Grow or go

Quite simply, I went into a situation familiar to most of us who love and lead the church. Institutional decline had left St. Bart's at a size not big enough and strong enough to be the people of God in our situation. I came to my work with a radical one-point program: church growth.

I don't believe you can read the New Testament and miss this basic truth. Jesus challenged those he called and taught to grow in spiritual maturity and depth. And he called followers to become leaders, and he left them with the tools they needed to spread the word and build the community. Paul and others brought a holy entrepreneurship to the building and growing process. The spiritual and practical message of the Gospel and the spread of the church was and is: grow or go.

Several "best practices" stand out, and one stands high above the others. The leader, and then the wider group of leaders, must believe unequivocally in growth. They must be tough and consistent in devising a strategy that subjects every decision and investment to that end. That's indispensable when the growth actually begins. The "you won't like it" part is simple reactivity to change. Many faithful leaders can stir up growth; only the non-anxious, non-reactive types can manage the backlash and keep growth going.

Some of the things I know will work:

+ **Invest ahead of the growth.** A scary and counterintuitive proposition for most vestry members, but there it is. Usually this will mean adding clergy and professional staff, and investing in quality music that is proportional to your need and consistent with your style.

+ **Do an audit of the blocks to people finding you and coming in —** from signage to publicity to quality of ushering. It's appalling how we often appear to be a small group having a good time with our arcane customs in a closed circle.

+ **Be candid and lovingly aggressive about stewardship of financial resources.** Teach and practice proportional giving for the personal, spiritual benefit it is. But don't avoid setting an annual, institutional goal — a real growth budget — and then work all year to get to it.

+ **Be transparent about what you believe** and teach the faith and local customs as attractively and continuously as you can. Nothing is less inviting to a seeker than to hear, "Sorry, you just missed the Inquirers' class, but there will be another next year."

✛ **Take a look at your governance structure and customs.** We've had to rethink vestry roles and processes twice in ten years. Clarify the difference between management and oversight. Staff and lead volunteers are the managers in all but the smallest congregations. The vestry must stick to oversight and, periodically, long-range planning for mission.

Above all, come together as leaders and work until you can adopt and believe in growth as an underlying goal and strategy. Make sure your leader preaches an "Our Dream" sermon at least once a year. And then back him or her when the growth starts — and when the whining begins.

Not with a bang but a whimper

Peter Drucker, in one of his basic management texts, speaks of "plastic moments" as "those periods that overlap when the old has gone but the new has not yet arrived and when the course of history is more open to being shaped and steered than any other time." The New Testament uses the word *kairos*. This is such a time for us. We know we must grow, or we will go — not with a bang but with a whimper no one will hear.

I believe the Episcopal Church is still useful to God. We have about seventy-five hundred local places who can prove that is true.

Marks of Vitality

WILLIAM L. SACHS

When the risen Christ appeared to two of his disciples on the road to Emmaus (Luke 24) their destination and their lives suddenly changed. Two millennia later the risen Christ still appears to his followers. The vivid experience of his presence alters their journeys as well. Not only are their lives made whole, their congregations are transformed. Today numerous Episcopalians discover the Emmaus road anew. The result is an unexpected burst of local vitality.

Soon after its Zacchaeus Project concluded, the Episcopal Church Foundation began its Emmaus Project. We determined to identify the sources of the vitality we had discovered in our Zacchaeus work. We believed that certain patterns of vitality could surface and could be linked to consistent forms of leadership in congregations and beyond. We wondered, what makes a congregation thrive? Broadly we concluded there must be a vivid sense of the risen Christ and an appreciative response. What happens when a church responds to a new sense of being led by Christ?

Findings from the Emmaus Project, sponsored by the Episcopal Church Foundation, indicate that vital congregations enthusiastically look beyond themselves, asking such questions as: What is the mission of this congregation, both locally and beyond? How can we grow in numbers, in our common life, and in service to others outside our doors?

So far the Emmaus Project has involved interviews with focus groups in nearly forty congregations in five dioceses. In addition we have spent time with the bishops and staffs of these dioceses and attended major diocesan events. We have also organized workshops on church life and leadership attended by dozens of people. Assessing what we have found, we are pleased to learn that the Zacchaeus Project's findings are being extended. Our understanding of what makes a congregation thrive now has greater definition.

Worship, Pastoral Care, and Education

"I remember when the diocese wanted to close this church. We couldn't get ten people out on a Sunday," recalled an older lay leader in one congregation. "Then the bishop sent us a new priest. He preached and he taught and he visited. And we began to grow." Clearly one mark of a thriving Episcopal church is capable guidance by clergy. The basis of church life lies in worship, pastoral care, and education. These tasks establish the foundation of the congregation's life. They must be faithfully sustained and energetically linked to the contours of local life.

Of course, local challenges can vary. One of the foremost marks of congregational vitality is the ability of ordained and lay leaders to formulate a mutually agreeable assessment of local demands and appropriate leadership styles. Yet certain consistent marks of congregational vitality readily appear, including:

✛ Ongoing development of leadership skills and the cultivation of new lay leaders.

✛ Regular, honest, affirmative forms of mutual ministry assessment. Regular forms of program review and long-range planning are included. These reviews stress the positive but do not deny or avoid attention to differences or tensions. Vital congregations look honestly at themselves.

✛ Life-giving connections to other parishes and to the diocese, and effective linkages to other groups that afford resources for the congregation's basic tasks such as worship, education, and pastoral care. Examples include Education for Ministry (EFM), Disciples of Christ in Community (DOCC), and Stephen Ministries. Vital congregations consistently are linked beyond themselves.

+ Ongoing attention to ways of integrating spiritual energies and questions into program life. Vital congregations consistently seek to embrace their members' needs and energies.

+ Sustained attention to the question of mission, i.e., what is the mission of this congregation, locally and beyond? How can the congregation grow, in numbers and in quality of common life, and in its service to others outside the congregation? We find that vital congregations enthusiastically look beyond themselves and ask how they can grow.

+ Last, vital congregations find ways to utilize conflict. They are able to face it honestly and to learn from it.

The Episcopal Church Foundation invites your contribution to the conversation on vitality and the leadership needed to encourage it. We look forward to meeting you on the Emmaus Road!

More Than Business as Usual: A Multicultural Scenario

LINDSAY HARDIN FREEMAN

Many parishes lock their doors by 12:00 noon on Sunday, the energy drained from the building. But for St. Nicholas Church in Noel, Missouri, a second surge of the day is just starting.

St. Nicholas is one of two congregations in the Diocese of West Missouri, and one of a growing number nationally, that is reaching out to new constituencies with new traditions — in St. Nicholas's case, a growing Latino community.

Six years ago, when the Reverend Barbara Beam arrived in Noel (population: 1,200), some twelve people, mostly elderly, sat in the pews. As in many small congregations, energy had ebbed and flowed over the years, and "ebb" seemed the operative word. But there were possibilities for evangelism in a growing local population of Latinos, many of whom worked at new chicken processing plants.

The parish developed some "traffic" during the week offering English classes for the workers and Spanish classes for those residents who wanted to better communicate with them. At the end of every class, Beam would say a prayer from the service of Compline. And from that start other things developed. Today, some twenty to thirty Latinos, about 40 percent of them children, gather at noon on Sunday. The effort has been a boom to both congregations, as the earlier 10:00 a.m. service remains stable and active.

Children are essential

Beam laughs as she describes the spontaneity of the service. "We come down from the altar, the crucifer and acolyte and I, and go to the back, and there's all these kids — with macarinas and tambourines — and we all process around the church, sometimes playing the last hymn two or three times."

Those children, she believes, are essential to the success of the ministry. "If the kids are involved and something is done on their behalf, the parents will keep coming."

Churches that are clear about their mission and purpose are more likely to be growing congregations. This relationship is consistent with all of the literature on church growth and vitality. Healthy churches know why they exist. They do not take their purpose of "being the church" for granted and evolve into social clubs with a chapel and chaplain.

— C. Kirk Hadaway, *A Report on Episcopal Churches in the United States*, 2002

Such an emphasis is essential if the Episcopal Church is to grow, believes C. Kirk Hadaway, director of research at the Episcopal Church Center. "The bottom line is this," he says in a recent report. "Given the demographic characteristics of our members, sustained growth is unlikely unless we begin to reach out beyond our historic constituency."

That constituency? Mostly white, older, well educated, and generally more affluent than the average American. Among mainline denominations, the Episcopal Church has the highest proportion of members who are college graduates and living in households earning $75,000 or more.

A lower birth rate for Episcopalians

While this sounds like a plus, there is a downside. More education and a higher income generally mean that women delay having children and have fewer of them. Episcopalians, in fact, have a much lower birth rate than the general population and bear fewer children on average than the members of almost all American denominations. And while more people join the Episcopal Church as adults than other mainline denominations, most are beyond their childbearing years.

Hadaway's conclusion is clear. "It will require much more than business as usual to expand into other constituencies."

Necessary anchors

Such growth and openness, says Canon Elizabeth Geitz, author of *Fireweed Evangelism,* may not always come easily. "I've never met a congregation that didn't want to grow, but the dynamics of accomplishing that growth are not always easy."

Geitz finds that before a congregation can be successful, welcoming newcomers into its midst, current parishioners must feel cared for and supported. Once "in-reach" programs such as pastoral care, education, etc. are in place, inclusion of new members is possible.

More specifically, Geitz points to a study of some fourteen thousand participants that identifies three sources of cohesion — heritage, vision, and moral commitment — which help congregations grow. If those anchors are present along with favorable demographics, then it may be time to reach out, to risk, to expand.

Slow but steady

Barbara Beam describes the small, sometimes awkward steps, in involving others. "When we first had new people in our church for language lessons, we offered them coffee," she said. But the coffee was on two different shelves, marked "church" and "classes."

"I took the signs down. We drank the same coffee. It was a small step, but it was a start."

Sometimes outreach has been of a different sort, like being asked to bless a truck. "What I love about these folks is how they want to involve the church in all they do," she says. "They will say, "Could you come and bless my truck? I need it for work."

And she does, working with the new while taking care of the old.

According to Kirk Hadaway, that kind of growth may change the demographics of the Episcopal Church in a startling way. "Even tiny gains across a denomination of seventy-three congregations would produce growth of a kind not seen since 1966," he says, referring to the high water mark of mainline denominational attendance. It will require much more than business as usual to expand into other constituencies. . . . It will take new churches and a new openness among our existing parishes."

Making Room for Newcomers

Ben Helmer

Church growth can be a revolving door experience. When a congregation masters the art of adding new members, it is often confronted with the issue of getting them to stay. Congregations both large and small experience the frustration of recruiting new members only to see them leave for another church home after a few months.

The first thing to remember is that this is reality for most growing churches. Not everyone will stay. Even the most successful growing congregations will admit this. The second thing to know is that the creation of an energetic membership base will take one of two forms: small churches "adopt" and large churches "incorporate" new members.

Adopt or incorporate

In the small church, adoption is the process by which new members are incorporated. This is a time of getting to know new members. New members should know they are being adopted when people start telling them about heroes (and villains!) in the congregation's history. The story is important. One congregation regularly sponsors a newcomers' night where veteran members are featured telling stories about the congregation and the people who have come before. A videotape of these stories is a wonderful way to preserve them and allow folks to take them home for private viewing.

Other parts of adoption include gradually involving new members in church activities and making room for them. The church that reserves active roles in worship and service to long-time members will not have a high adoption rate. However, the church that makes a new member senior warden after a year puts that new member in a precarious role and may be looking for another one at the next annual meeting! Common sense and good follow-up are the norms for adoption. Work at it. It doesn't happen by accident.

Incorporation in larger churches usually comes through involvement in activities. People charged with introducing prospective new members to the programs and small groups offered by the congregation are essential. If new members have to do all the investigating and asking, they will probably assume membership is a "secret process" from which they are excluded. This is when people often decide to look elsewhere.

Pro or con subliminal messages?

What subliminal messages does your church convey? At announcement time are different voices heard inviting new people to attend an event?

Things Best Left Unsaid

We admit to having a little fun here at Vestry Papers *and came up with the following list of things NOT to say to prospective members. Try making your own list as a warm-up to a serious conversation of how best to sustain new members.*

✛ Would you help with the rummage sale? It's pretty dusty downstairs, but that's where we start the new people off.

✛ You can't sit in that pew — it belongs to the Schmidlach family. And that one over there? No, that's the wrong pew, too.

✛ We'd like you to wear this red target on your forehead so everyone will know you're new.

✛ Oh, we're so glad you're here. We need your pledge money right away.

✛ Would you like to join the vestry? We could really use a new senior warden.

✛ The bathroom? Just right down that hallway, take a left at the steps, then down two flights. Toilet paper. Maybe.

✛ Jump right in, introverts — stand up and introduce yourselves!

✛ Here's what you'll need for the service: our leaflet, the readings, the Prayer Book, the hymnal, the supplemental text, and the announcements.

✛ Oh, thank God, fresh blood.

✛ Gee, we haven't had a young family like you in forever.

✛ The Hispanic church is just down the street.

✛ A nursery? Maybe in a couple of months if more people show up.

✛ Of course you can't be on the outreach committee. You haven't been here long enough.

Are new members invited to a small group or activity and welcomed as potential participants? Are youth and young people's programs open for growth?

Successful growing churches, regardless of size, admit they have changed dramatically in their time of growth, and they expect to keep changing as they grow.

Research tells us that members of a church today are not as interested in brand loyalty as they once were. They will find a church that suits their needs and meets their expectations with less regard to whether it's the Episcopal Church or another denomination. So the implications are that the congregation has to listen and be ready to shift priorities, responding to needs of new cultures and new times. Successful growing churches, regardless of size, admit they have changed dramatically in their time of growth, and they expect to keep changing as they grow. That always means some people will leave rather than change to accommodate the needs of new members.

A good formation tool is essential to incorporating new members who will stay. An ongoing program that teaches the basics of the faith, is a safe place to ask questions, and insists on "you" being more important than "us" is vital. Large congregations can usually have an ongoing small group for new members. Small churches may need to have them as demand requires. The essentials of this are that long-time members come together with new ones in a climate where both learn together.

A commitment to mission is essential

A common thread among all growing churches is their ability to connect membership with mission. People respond well to opportunities for engaging with others in a common ministry to their community and the world. They also appreciate the church recognizing and affirming their daily life and work as part of its mission. Programs about parenting, the work place, and related daily living are key to retaining members.

If you visit a church that is growing, members will usually share two things about why they grow:

✚ Everyone has gifts and those gifts are identified and nurtured;

✚ Everyone has ministries from Sunday to Saturday that are important and need to be affirmed.

Outward and Visible Signs:
A Sunday Checklist

Welcoming guests to your congregation is somewhat like a sacrament—an outward and visible sign of an inward and spiritual grace. So open the front doors and take a walk through your church. Try to feel what a newcomer would experience. Or better yet, take a guest with you and listen to what he or she has to say.

Approaching the church

❑ Are the service times posted outside?

❑ Are they accurate and readable, not blocked by bushes?

❑ Is there an easy way to get directions via phone or Web site?

❑ Do the grounds reflect that people care?

❑ Are there spaces for guest parking?

Walking in

❑ Does the door open easily? Is it free of peeling paint and cobwebs?

❑ Is the entryway clean and free of clutter? (Old jackets, snow shovels, coffee cups, etc.)

❑ Is there an usher, a vestry member, and/or clergy saying hello?

❑ Are there signs to bathrooms? Are the bathrooms clean?

❑ Are there signs to the church school and nursery?

❑ Is there a guest book or a sign-in system?

❑ Is there written information on the church?

The service

❑ Is the Sunday bulletin understandable?

❑ Are instructions clear for receiving Communion, etc.?

❑ Are guests welcomed during the service? Helped if looking lost?

❑ Is there a level of vitality that would be attractive?

The nursery

❑ Is the nursery well-marked? Would you feel safe leaving your baby there?

❑ Is the nursery cleaned regularly? Is it cheerful?

❑ Is the nursery caregiver-friendly?

❑ Is there a way for parents to be reached if, for example, their babies are crying uncontrollably?

❑ Are there snacks? Diapers?

❑ Are there clean toys and books? Often nurseries can be dumping grounds for grimy toys and dog-eared books.

The church school

❑ Are there signs pointing to the church school?

❑ May children join throughout the year?

❑ Are parents welcome to observe?

❑ Is there a greeter to say hello and answer questions?

❑ Is there information available regarding curriculum?

❑ Is there energy in the rooms? Does it look like there is new life?

After church

❑ Is the coffee good enough to serve guests in the Lord's house?

❑ Are guests greeted in a friendly but not overbearing manner?

❑ How about visual aids? Bulletin boards of current events and photos of vestry members and staff are helpful.

❑ Decent munchies?

❑ Are copies of the parish newsletter out for people to pick up?

❑ Can guests get nametags, too, if members wear them?

❑ Is there a system for following up with those who have come?

Being about God's business

The life of a healthy congregation is built on the needs of its members and the vision of its mission. When membership and healthy relationships form the core of the congregation's life, the vision is continually refreshed and renewed. Jesus began his public ministry with a clear and somewhat narrow view of what it encompassed. He ended it with an awareness of the Father's love for all humanity, not just the Jews. If we are truly about God's business — loving souls and mending broken hearts — what we have to offer will only be expanded by what we receive from those whom God sends to us.

TWO

The Ministry of Hospitality

I was a stranger and you welcomed me.
— Matthew 25:35

Once your vestry has committed itself to church growth, the next step is to walk through your doors — from a guest's point of view. What lurks inside the entryway? Cobwebs and old coffee cups? Shovels and brooms? Or friendly people and inviting literature? And as writer George Martin says, good coffee helps.

How about the congregation? To have a truly effective ministry of hospitality, all groups within the parish need to be active in reaching out to newcomers. If the underlying culture is one of being suspicious of visitors, whether it be that first Sunday or when children enroll in church school, it will be obvious — and disheartening.

Saying hello is perhaps the easiest part. And then once hello is said, it's a bit of a Pandora's box. What if we don't like who walks in the door? Well, God didn't say anything about liking them. What if they don't understand how we do things? They probably won't. What if they speak a different language? They might. What if we have to change? *No, I don't think so.*

Unfortunately, saying no to change isn't part of our biblical history as Christians. Well, maybe it is. It's just that people who say no usually don't get the chance to go ahead, to grow, to enter the Promised Land. Often it is those congregations who grow stale and eventually wither.

From Moses to Rahab to Jesus to Paul, change has been as integral to health and growth as free speech is to a democracy. So let's be clear: saying "hello" in church may well begin a process of change. We may or may not like it, but as God's people, it is what we are meant to do.

41

Entertaining Angels Unaware

Elizabeth R. Geitz

Do not neglect to show hospitality to strangers, for by doing that some have entertained angels without knowing it.   —Hebrews 13:2

Are you entertaining angels? When I work with vestries on hospitality ministry, this is the first question I ask. Why? I repeatedly hear, "Our newcomer program just fizzled out"; "we can't find anyone to lead it"; or "we have a committee but we aren't getting anywhere."

Central to a flourishing and sustainable hospitality program is a clear understanding of why we, as Christians, are engaged in it. Why is hospitality a ministry and what marks Christian hospitality as unique?

Within first-century Judaism, Abraham was heralded as the supreme practitioner of hospitality. In Genesis, he and Sarah reach out in hospitality to three heavenly strangers, offering them a meal. While they are eating, one gives them a message that could only have come from God.

A few years prior to Jesus' ministry, a large monument was erected by Herod the Great on the site of this meeting, highlighting its centrality within the Jewish tradition. First-century Jews believed that the way they received the stranger was how God would receive them at the great end-time banquet.

Left out or welcomed?

What if God receives us in the same way we have received those God sends to us? At the Great Coffee Hour in the Sky will we be sitting on the side, feeling left out and alone? Or will we be welcomed with open arms by those who are already comfortably in?

These questions give me much to ponder, for in my years as a vestry member, I often used coffee hour as a time to catch up on what I thought was the "serious" business of the church. How wrong I was! It was not only my responsibility as a leader to reach out to others in the name of Christ, but to model that behavior for other members of the congregation.

Hospitality to the stranger was not only central to first-century Jewish and Christian belief; both religions are dependent on hospitality for their very existence.

The Jewish faith was shared by traveling teachers, who were dependent on the hospitality of those who welcomed them into their homes. Jesus traveled to spread the Good News and often stayed in people's homes, sharing his wisdom with those who warmly received him.

Similarly, Paul traveled and taught in homes. As hospitality was extended, the good news was proclaimed. Without such welcoming, the

Gospel message might never have spread beyond the boundaries of Palestine.

Seeing ourselves as part of this ongoing tradition is the first step toward understanding hospitality as ministry. The second step is understanding the uniqueness of Christian hospitality.

Who is the stranger?

At the heart of hospitality is welcoming the stranger, but who is the stranger? In the movie *Sister Act,* Whoopi Goldberg plays the role of a nightclub singer who witnesses a murder. As a result, her life is in danger. For protection, she is taken to a convent and directed to the mother superior's study. Before the mother superior enters, a monsignor informs her of Whoopi's predicament. The mother superior agrees to accept Whoopi, until she opens the door and sees her wearing a gold lamé coat, a purple-sequined outfit, and a profusion of jewelry. The mother superior gasps and shuts the door. The monsignor reminds her, in not-so-gentle tones, "You have taken a vow of hospitality to all in need." With a straight face, the mother superior replies, "I lied."

"When did we see a stranger and welcome thee, or naked and clothe thee? And when did we see thee sick or in prison and visit thee?" And Jesus answered, "Truly I say to you, as you did it to one of the least of these, you did it to me."

—Matthew 25:38–40

How often do we, upon seeing the strangers God sends our way, say somewhere in our heart, "I lied. I lied when I took my baptismal vows and promised to seek and serve Christ in all persons and to respect the dignity of every human being."

Yet the first distinction of Christian hospitality is precisely that we welcome those who may be unwelcome in other settings. Jesus' hospitality to those who were unwelcome or deemed unacceptable was a hallmark of his ministry. If we extend hospitality in the name of Christ we are meant to do no less.

The second distinction of Christian hospitality is that those who welcome the stranger often receive far more than they give. When we reach out to someone in the name of Christ, Christ is often present in profound and deeply moving ways. It is this awareness of Christ's presence that enables us to be not only hosts to the stranger, but guests of the stranger as well.

I saw a stranger yestreen;
I put food in the eating place,
Drink in the drinking place,
Music in the listening place;
And in the blessed name of the Triune
he blessed myself and my house,
my cattle and my dear ones.
And the lark said in her song
Often, often, often,
Goes the Christ in the stranger's guise;
Often, often, often,
Goes the Christ in the stranger's guise.

—from an old Gaelic poem

A greater awareness of the true meaning of Christian hospitality will transform you and the life of your church for years to come.

Radical Hospitality:
Crossing the Cultural Divide

ANTHONY GUILLÉN

Maria, a young girl of seven, has just served herself some coffee at our coffee hour. She adds spoon after spoon of sugar and soon will be adding about the same amount of creamer to her cup.

Some long-time members of this parish are indignant that this child is not being supervised. They comment on how wasteful the child is being and wonder where her parents are. One of them snatches the cup of coffee out of Maria's hand and scolds her for using too much sugar.

"And besides, you're too young to be drinking coffee," the parishioner says. The little girl seems puzzled as she looks for support from her parents, who are now standing beside her. They explain that she must leave the coffee alone. The parents glance around the room, apologize to the offended parishioners, and leave.

This scenario is all too familiar with many clergy and laity alike who are involved in multicultural ministry. It might not be about children drinking coffee — which is common for children to do in Latino homes, thus the carryover at church — but the issue is about insensitivity and ignorance about cultural norms. I am amazed at how often little or no thought has gone into cultural awareness as the welcoming parish sets out to invite another group into its midst. In our case, I prided myself on the fact that we did a lot of preparation in anticipation for our bold step. What could possibly go wrong?

A conscious decision

All Saints made a conscious decision to embark on a ministry to the Latino community in Oxnard ten years ago when I arrived. Our target population was the many unchurched Latinos in our community. Demographics had changed dramatically, and Latinos made up about 74 percent of the population. When I arrived, the majority of our parishioners were Anglo. The vestry was clear that we needed to reach out to the community for two reasons: the Gospel mandate and the reality of a graying congregation. We were aware that there might be opposition from some parishioners, and that some might leave the parish as a result. So we prayed, discussed the challenges before us, and addressed the cultural norms that we would be facing.

We then shared our vision of what we hoped would occur and things that might be problematic. Feeling confident that we had done our homework, we opened our hearts and the doors to the Latino community.

We first hired a youth minister, initiated several after-school programs, and offered first communion classes. It was our hope that once we attracted the children their parents would follow. And indeed by the grace of God we were successful. However our success was also the cause of some major problems.

> *We have noted that the large, evangelical church nearby saves about five Sunday parking spots near the front door for guests, and urges its own members to park farther away. Episcopalians, take note! It seems like a welcoming thing to do.*

Soon our Sunday school classes were overflowing. But we had difficulty recruiting teachers, especially teachers who were bilingual. And while there was new energy and vitality, some of the children of parishioners felt their classrooms had been taken over by newcomers and were refusing to attend. We should have prepared the children and their parents to receive these newcomers into their classrooms, which we did not do.

We had originally scheduled our Spanish Eucharist for 9:30 a.m., between the two English services at 8:00 a.m. and 11:00 a.m. Because of the proximity of the services, however, parishioners complained that they could not find parking spaces or empty seats in the parish hall. Coffee hour supplies ran short and expenses went up.

Finally, the issue of culture caused some consternation, especially for those who attended the late English Eucharist. Latinos have a different view of time, and our 9:30 Eucharist was regularly starting late and thus affecting the eleven o'clockers. (Our Spanish Mass is now held at noon and we no longer face this headache.)

Not ready for all the changes

Was everything as bad as I have just painted it? Of course not. All Saints is truly a very hospitable and friendly congregation. We simply were not ready for all the changes that were required of us and we did not anticipate some of the problems that arose.

Yes, there were some parishioners who were not keen on sharing their church and their priest and probably subconsciously demonstrated that to the Latinos by the way they looked at or treated them. And yes, we did lose some of the newcomers because they perceived that they were not welcome.

But today we are a very different community. We have children in the nursery and in church. We worship in two languages, occasionally holding bilingual services. Our new chapel is dedicated to Our Lady of Guadalupe. Anglos and Latinos serve on the vestry, are delegates to diocesan convention, and financially support the life of the church. Together our new community celebrates Shrove Tuesday and Thanksgiving Day along with Día de los Muertos (Day of the Dead celebration) and Posadas (a Christmas tradition).

All Saints celebrates the richness of our diversity. We, like many parishes in our diocese and around our church, are bilingual/bicultural or multilingual/multicultural/multiethnic. We are not the future face of the church; we are already what the church looks, sounds, and tastes like.

Hospitality Matters:
Seeing Our Buildings Anew

ELIZA LINLEY

Episcopalians have moved beyond the era when, as the old joke went, evangelism meant unlocking the door on Sunday mornings. But how often does force of habit make us blind to our worship environment — without regard to design flaws and neglect that give a negative message?

If we believe that hospitality is a Gospel mandate, it is part of the mission of the church to look at our buildings with fresh eyes, to take an inventory, and to take care of the things that need attention. In terms of facilities, hospitality translates into four categories: safety, accessibility, comfort, and attractiveness. Let's look from the outside in, with Sunday morning as the focus.

The approach

✚ Is the church pleasing to look at? Besides general maintenance, does the landscaping enhance the building or hide it? Does shrubbery encroach on entry walkways, signs, exterior lighting, or windows? Attention to detail and bright plantings near the entry draws attention to it, and to the changing church seasons.

✚ Are walkways and entries clear and easy to negotiate? Or have roots, settlement, or frost heaves created broken slabs and safety hazards? In facility triage, safety needs have highest priority. If they can't be fixed immediately, slippery walkways and steps should be highlighted with tape, paint, or nonskid coatings.

✚ Is it clear where to park? While spaces for the disabled are mandated by law, not all churches remember to mark a few convenient parking spaces "reserved for visitors."

✚ Are signs clear and well coordinated? Or is the church sign that was so nice twenty years ago in need of replacement or new paint? Can new parents find the nursery? Are restrooms and offices clearly marked?

✚ How hard is it to enter by a wheelchair, crutches, or a stroller? It's not enough to provide access if it can't be found, or if you need assistance to negotiate it.

The entry

✚ Visitors should be able to see inside the building as they approach. At the very least, a pair of wide-open doors into a well-lit entry helps.

✚ The entry area, or narthex, needs to be attractive and constantly monitored to keep clutter down. Does the visual serenity of your entry enhance a sense of calm and reverence? Or is it the repository of lost umbrellas, galoshes, hats and coats, dusty hymnals, errant crayons, out-of-date postings, dying plants, and boxes? Be ruthless.

✚ Post things elsewhere. Leave space for the visitors' book, bulletins for one service only, copies of the church newsletter, and large-print prayer books and hymnals.

The sanctuary

✚ Can everyone see clearly? Quality lighting can really "pop out" a handsome old building. New lighting may also be more energy-efficient. A good lighting consultant is well worth the expense. It is not always necessary to replace old fixtures — it may be possible to augment the system and relamp instead.

+ Does the seating work for everyone? Is space allowed for wheelchairs? Do little people have to peer over pews? Some churches have made the front row of seating into kid-friendly soft cushions on the floor. If seating is so uncomfortable as to be a hindrance to worship, consider replacement.

+ How are the acoustics? Bad acoustics discourage people from singing. Sound does not turn corners. An acoustical consultant can help find solutions, including more resonant surfaces, baffles, and sensitive amplification.

I was glad when they said to me,
"Let us go to the house of the Lord."
                                        —Psalm 122:1

+ Is the floor covering dangerously worn? Torn, frayed, or bunched carpets are a safety hazard. Old softwood pews can splinter: repair them.

+ People with chemical and environmental sensitivities are miserable in buildings where there is perfume, incense, or poor ventilation. Some churches ask parishioners not to wear scent. If incense is used for a special service, can the sanctuary be fully opened and ventilated in time for the next event?

+ As in the entry, strive to minimize visual clutter. One cross is enough; more diminish the primacy of the symbol. Think hard about how much "stuff" you need. Less is more.

+ Is your color scheme stuck in a 1960s beige syndrome? Paint and finishes can be brought up to date, brightened, and made richer for a comparatively moderate outlay.

In short, church is like home. When it is warm, inviting, and safe, we all feel better. When company is coming, you want them to feel neither intimidated nor discouraged, but at home. And at church, company is always coming. The welcome our buildings extend should mirror God's love. Our church facilities should be places from which we go to do the things the Gospel asks us to do. Is this too big a charge? Maybe that's okay. Keep the larger goal in mind, and a task list that may seem daunting starts to look more like an opportunity for faithful, even joyful ministry. After all, the church is God's house. Can we do any less?

Are They Visitors or Guests?

George Martin

Have you ever walked into a Wal-Mart about 9 o'clock at night? Even at that hour, chances are that there will be a greeter at the door who smiles at you and offers you a shopping cart. Sure, you could get one yourself. You know all about wrenching the last cart when it is stuck to a long line, but at Wal-Mart you take the offered cart and start shopping.

Wouldn't it be nice if we greeted people at church in the same way? We don't need to give people a shopping cart, but the analogy shouldn't be lost on us. Chances are that folks have come to church looking for something that is meaningful and lasting — maybe even something that is eternal. But even if folks don't have such long-range goals in mind, if we simply greet those first-time guests with a smile and offer to help them find seats, we may actually start a process that will lead them to come back again and again.

Most people come to a church because they were invited by a neighbor, friend, or family member. Sponsor regular "Bring a Friend to Church" Sundays. Make it fun. Remember that young people move in crowds. Have food, decent coffee, even prizes — besides eternal life, that is.

Please notice, by the way, that I've talked about welcoming guests. What a difference between treating someone as a visitor and treating that person as a guest! The former is a tourist, while the latter is more like a member of the family. Very few of us, for example, have *visitor rooms* in our homes, but many of us have a guest room. A guest is a special person in our home who is often given kitchen privileges, who often gets to stay for more than a single night, and who may even be given a key to the house.

What about your church? Do you have little cards in the pews for your visitors? Do you thank your visitors for being with you? If that's what you're calling them, are you thinking that they won't come again, and that you'll have a different group of visitors to welcome next week? *That's the trouble with the term "visitors."*

Examining our ministry to guests

These questions force us to examine what our business is when it comes to welcoming people who are new to the church. If your church is serious

49

about having guests, especially the kind who really end up getting their own keys, then this emphasis will be visible and clear to all. Guest ministry is essential, needs to begin with the vestry, and should show up in the church's budget.

Ever seen an ad suggesting how much fun it might be to come to a Disney park? Ever seen that smiley face on TV cutting prices at Wal-Mart? Chances are we've all seen these ads, and that's because each company invests money in advertising. What does your church budget say about welcoming guests? Have you budgeted money so that you'll increase the likelihood of people coming to your church? Think of money that is budgeted for advertising as an investment in a guest ministry meant to pay dividends in the lives of those you welcome.

August is a surprisingly popular month for "church shopping." Plan to have greeters and materials ready to go, rather than waiting for September. That way, newcomers are on board for the start of fall activities.

Then there is the matter of what we actually do when Sunday morning arrives. I suggest we begin with signs that say "Guests Expected!" What if the vestry followed the Wal-Mart principle, with the clergy and/or vestry members at the front door each and every week? (Hint: if you have more than one service, let vestry people serve at the service they prefer to attend.)

If we want to extend the logic of this ministry even further, we should also be concerned with a whole range of things which could make that first church experience as pleasant and as memorable as possible. You might want to start asking if your worship really is as easy to follow as you think it is. (Put the whole thing in a bulletin, including prayers, and hymns, and it will be totally user-friendly.)

Improve the coffee and conversation

If you want to really get serious about this ministry, you might also want to think about the quality of the coffee that is served after church — and look at your budget item for coffee. Few people seem to be asking for coffee that has a slight metallic flavor left in it, but that's what you can find at many a church! Upgrading your coffee makers and the kind of coffee you brew might pay dividends. What's really needed, of course, are people who will talk to our guests during those social times. Once again, members of the vestry can decide to take the leadership on this matter.

Bishop Payne says that "an engaging, open and loving aggressive church culture is a prerequisite for health" (see p. 27 above). Good words. Let's be engaging, open, and loving. Let's also be aggressive, at least in the sense that we will go out of our way to welcome those who come.

We won't simply expect them to find their own place and we certainly won't treat them as if they are visitors whom we will never see again. On the contrary, let's invest in those guests in such a way that they will always know that they received a genuine and sincere welcome when they came to the Episcopal Church. If we take this ministry seriously, we may finally understand what God means about welcoming strangers and discovering that God really is sending us angels.

Outward and Visible Signs:
Following up with Prospective Members

Elizabeth Geitz

Enlarge the site of your tent, and let the curtains of your habitations be stretched out; do not hold back; lengthen your cords and strengthen your stakes.   —Isaiah 54:2

To enlarge the site of our tent today requires intentional follow-up on initial visits. If a comprehensive system is not in place we will lose the many angels God sends to worship with us.

Following up on initial visits

❑ Do you treat every newcomer as an angel sent by God?

❑ If the guest is of a different ethnic origin than the majority of your congregation, do you have in place an intentional way of listening "with the ear of the heart" to your guests particular needs?

❑ Is your congregation educated about the needs of different ethnic groups within your community?

❑ Do you obtain the name and address of every guest who worships in your church?

❑ Do you have a lay calling system?

❑ Are people visited within thirty-six hours of attending your church?

❑ Is there a record-keeping system in place?

❑ Do you assign a shepherd to each newcomer for one to two years?

Orienting and integrating new members

❑ Does your church offer a newcomer forum outlining church programs and offerings?

❑ Do you host several parties a year for new members?

❑ Are these gatherings offered at different times of the day and week to attract a diverse population?

❑ Are there clear guidelines to help someone become a member of your parish?

❑ Do you offer a new member dedication litany during a worship service?

❑ Does your church assign baptismal sponsors to new families who seek the church for baptism of a child?

❑ Is Guild of the Christ Child used in your parish?*

❑ Do you have a structure in place for new members to deepen and share their faith with one another?

❑ Is there a system to integrate new members into small groups?

❑ Is there a system designed to help them move into leadership roles?

❑ Do you follow up with new members at the one-year mark?

❑ Is there a way for new members to give feedback to the hospitality committee and clergy about their experience of joining your congregation?

---

*Guild of the Christ Child is a program that provides two-year follow-up for parents of the newly baptized with letters and cards to send to the new parents at anniversaries, keeping them connected to the church. For more information, call (503) 223-4171.

THREE

Vestry Roles and Responsibilities

[And Moses said:] "I am not able to carry all this people alone, for they are too heavy for me...." So the Lord said to Moses, "Gather for me seventy of the elders of Israel.... Bring them to the tent of meeting, and have them take their place there with you."
— Numbers 11:14–16

Defining the actual role of a vestry, and of the individual vestry members, is paradoxically one of the trickier items of church business. We bring many models to the role from our outside lives: boards of directors, employer-employee relations relative to the clergy and staff, volunteer committees of various types, and more.

In fact, none of these exactly fits, as the vestry model is a unique one, reflecting the spiritual nature of the enterprise, the hierarchical nature of Episcopal Church, and a unique partnership reality between vestries and rectors.

This last is perhaps most important because, at least on paper, national canons (church law) say very little about the roles and responsibilities of vestries beyond being legal agents and representatives of a parish, while assigning lots of responsibility and authority for the pastoral and spiritual direction of a congregation to rectors.

In practice, no one person can carry out all those responsibilities without significant help and support, and thus a significant part of a vestry's actual life roles—its working structure and relationships—comes out of the realities of its particular congregational situation. In some congregations, a very corporate, hands-off, oversight approach will be appropriate. In others, hands-on involvement is simply essential.

In virtually all cases, as our authors point out, *the vestry journey is a spiritual enterprise*—on both a personal and a group level. A partnership between the rector and the vestry will be the best way forward. Intentional focus on being missionaries and attention to one's own spiritual life is enormously helpful, as is developing a positive collaboration of mutual support.

Vestry Responsibilities: My Top Ten List

Scott Evenbeck

Just as the Great Commission — "Go therefore into the world to make disciples of all nations" — does not go into great detail on how exactly to accomplish that mission, so to the canons of the Episcopal Church are not particularly specific about the responsibilities of vestries.

The vestry "shall be agents and legal representatives of the Parish in all matters concerning its corporate property and the relations of the parish to its clergy" (Canon 14). That's the whole thing.

Being from David Letterman's Indiana hometown (I used to shop at the store where he carried out groceries) and to provide a little more meat on the bones of how a vestry ought to act, I offer here my Top Ten list of how I understand the responsibilities of vestries:

1. Those of us on vestries should explicitly seek God's guidance in our work. While a vestry has legal and fiscal responsibilities (and must take them seriously), a vestry is not a board of directors for a business or a not-for-profit organization. The work of the vestry can be done only as it is grounded in the Spirit. Too often we are not intentional and reflective about our work.

How then do we remind ourselves that the work of the vestry is God's work? We might light a candle to remind us of the presence of Christ. We might end the meetings with Compline. We might share spiritual reflections as a regular part of the agenda. We do begin and end the meetings with prayer.

2. The vestry must seek means to form community. A vestry is a group of individuals, called to work in the church, together. Most likely, vestry members will come from different services with different backgrounds and have various agendas. Finding common ground, centered on the spiritual life of individuals and of the vestry as a group, then, is fundamental to successful work as a vestry.

3. A vestry should act in concert with the rector. The rector is a member of the vestry. The rector chairs the vestry. The rector has canonical authority (e.g., use of space) for certain matters in the church. The rector is *not* a CEO hired by a board of directors to direct a staff carrying out the mandates of the board. Rather the rector is a *partner* with the vestry in the mutual discernment of mission.

In concert with the bishop, the vestry determines the means for calling the rector and negotiating a memorandum of agreement. But after that, it's a partnership.

4. The vestry is not a representative body. Thinking of vestry membership as one from Christian education, one from the choir, one from the Scouts, etc., where we vote *our* interests, will only get us into trouble.

The vestry is a group of individuals seeking to discern, with the rector, what the parish is called to do and to have oversight of that work.

5. A vestry must define its *own* mission, vision, values, and goals. There are many organizing principles for outlining the work of the vestry. Personally I like the SWEEPS model (stewardship, worship, education, evangelism, pastoral care, and service), partly because the acronym is memorable.

But what is more important is that the vestry moves away from automatic pilot to define its own direction. Vestries are well served by being intentional about their agenda and work.

There are many ways to share in the spiritual leadership of parishes, not the least of which is coming to church every Sunday. Speak of your faith publicly, in church and at work. Teach a class. Be a missionary in your daily life. Pray for your parish, the clergy, your ministry, and the vestry.

---

6. Vestries must set strict time limits on buildings and grounds discussions. Vestries, in my experience, often move their attention to the concrete.

It is a lot easier to spend a year's worth of meetings hashing out the problems with the old carpet (which people may trip on as they enter meetings) than it is to decide to *fix* the carpet and move on to what the parish is called to do. Set strict time limits on buildings and grounds discussions, form a committee — and get on with attending to the rest of the life of the church.

7. Hold yourself, and one another, accountable. Have vestry members committed to the tithe as the standard for giving? Does anyone talk about pledging in concrete terms?

The last vestry on which I served would probably have exceeded the giving of the entire parish if the vestry members had approached a "modern" tithe of 5 percent, let alone the biblical tithe. My own parish reinforces that a person's pledge is known only to the bookkeeper, not to the rector or anyone else. That sure keeps stewardship in the closet.

8. Vestries should celebrate. Annual picnics, receptions, outings, dinners, and other celebratory events should be part of vestry life.

9. Vestries should have formal rituals. We're a liturgical church. We like this stuff. It's meaningful to us. Begin (and maybe end) service on the vestry with a formal ritual in a worship service. It's what we do well. And it matters.

10. Vestries should seek continuity and embrace change. In many parishes, the "old guard" controls the vestry. In others, there is so much turnover that the continuity that allows for living out a mission is lost, with the parish reinventing itself every year. It is a delicate balance — to provide continuity and to bring in "new blood" and new ideas. But it's a balance we need to constantly work on. And being about balance — it's even Anglican!

Easing the Load: Missionaries One and All

A. Wayne Schwab

Is not God most concerned about how we live from Monday to Saturday? Are not Sunday and all of church life intended to provide guidance and power for our Monday to Saturday living? Therefore, congregations appropriately make their basic purpose that of supporting the members in their daily living as Christians.

The vestry does not legislate this purpose by a resolution. Rather, vestry and clergy together lead the congregation into living it. It takes time. It looks difficult, but as congregational life moves toward this goal, vestry members feel the weight of leadership decrease. Their yoke becomes easier and their burden becomes lighter.

Unexpected missionaries

The change begins with the vestry. They look at what they are doing to make life better — more loving, more fair — in each area of their daily lives. Next, they discover that what they work to accomplish God is working to accomplish with them. They are missionaries — agents of God's mission — and did not know it!

Their homes, their work, their local communities, the wider world, and their recreation, as well as the church are their "mission fields." These six areas are the places — the "mission fields" — where they work with God to make life better.

They had thought they would run the "business side" of the church, help the clergy get "jobs" done, and recruit members to help them. They find, instead, that their real task is to help the members discover their daily missions and live them well. And the vestry's work is far more rewarding as the members rejoice over being met where they are — in their daily living.

Reflection is key

How does this new kind of leadership occur? In hour-long sessions with small groups of six to eight, vestry teams lead members in reflecting on one of the six daily mission fields:*

+ What is God doing in this part of my life now?

+ What inhibits God's love and justice there?

+ What change is needed?

+ Knowing my own gifts, what will I do there to make life better?

+ How will I get others to help me?

+ How will I talk of God and being "fed" — empowered — at Jesus' table while we work together?

As members begin to see that God is working with them in one of their mission fields, they want to explore the other five as well. They enjoy discovering that they, too, are missionaries. And the vestry members enjoy deeper bonding with the people than they have ever known.

This works because God is on mission in the world everywhere, every moment to overcome whatever blocks love and justice — the public face of love. God's mission has a church. The church does not have a mission. The church is the visible instrument of God's mission. We join God's mission in baptism as we commit ourselves to make Jesus Christ known in deed and word, to love neighbor as self, and to strive for peace and justice — all with God's help.

Some examples of changes this new leadership brings:

Newcomers and people seeking baptism or deeper commitment discover their own daily missions and find that the congregation is there to support them in their missions. They soon discover they are not on the edge of God's mission, but at its center.

Sunday worship affirms the daily missions of the members. The Prayers of the People are reworded to invite specific petitions and thanksgivings in silence or aloud. The intercessor waits until silence suggests all have had their chance. Vestry members offer prayers about their own work, the local community, the wider world, and their leisure. In time, the rest offer their own prayers, and this time becomes more truly the prayers of the people.

---

*For specific methods, see Appendixes A and C of the author's *When the Members Are the Missionaries: An Extraordinary Calling for Ordinary People*, published by Member Mission Press.

In a mission-centered church school, the teachers meet the children and youth as peers. All are baptized agents of the mission of Jesus Christ. Classes begin with the Gospel, move to how it calls us to live, and end with what to ask God for to live this way. Teachers are easier to recruit because they see their knowledge of life, not church matters, is what counts.

Conflicts are easier to resolve when the congregation's purpose is supporting the members in their daily living. "Big" conflicts assume their proper proportions, and compromises, while never pain-free, are easier to reach. Differences on worship, teaching, and program are settled on the basis of what best supports the members in their daily living.

Staffing those onerous tasks few want to assume is easier when leaders can relate them to enabling the daily missions of the members. The mission field of church has its nitty-gritty jobs just like the other mission fields — from doing the dishes to improving communication.

> *It is not for you to know the times or periods that the Father has set by his own authority. But you will receive power when the Holy Spirit has come upon you; and you will be my witnesses . . . to the ends of the earth.*   —Acts 1:7–8

Knowing stewardship is more than meeting a budget, one congregation will start their fall canvass in the spring. Every household will be asked by phone to give two concrete ways the church can serve them better in "their personal mission fields of home, neighborhood, workplace, and wider world." The results, then, shape next year's program.

For evangelism, discerning daily missions by vestry and parishioners includes how each draws others into their mission, and how each will talk of God's mission with the new teammates and invite them along to Jesus' table. All have looked into the heart of the best of evangelism — bringing good news in deed and word into every arena of daily life.

Who Are We, the Vestry?

Linda Grenz

A congregation is led by its clergy and vestry. This is not a board of directors, nor is it a senior management team, though there are some similarities in the ways these various groups function. A vestry is different because the church is different. We can only understand the peculiarities of vestry identity when we see that identity in the context of the church, the setting in which the vestry exercises its ministry of leadership.

Clergy and laity both have vital roles in the leadership of the church. Though the rector and the vestry have somewhat different responsibilities (as described in the material that follows), a trusting relationship enables them to work closely together. Trust should characterize their relationship.

The catechism in the Book of Common Prayer (page 855) sets forth the church's reason for being: it is to restore people to unity with God and each other in Christ. Our primary task is reconciliation. As individuals and as communities, we carry out that mission as we "represent Christ and his Church; bear witness to him wherever [we] may be; and, according to gifts given [us], carry on Christ's work of reconciliation in the world; and take [our] place in the life, worship and governance of the Church."

The vestry is . . .

The vestry is the body within a congregation that, with the clergy, leads the parish. The vestry:

+ helps to discern the vision toward which God is drawing that particular community;

+ articulates and communicates the vision;

+ holds the community accountable for its realization of that vision; and

+ keeps the mission of the church and that of the individual congregation clearly before the parish community.

The canons of the church actually have very little to say about the roles and responsibilities of vestries per se. Broadly speaking, they specify responsibilities for the stewardship of money and property, and then two other areas that overlap with clergy responsibilities — personnel management, and program development and oversight.

This article was excerpted from "Who Are We, the Vestry?" in *The Vestry Resource Guide: Servants Called to Leadership*, 2001, by Linda Grenz, published by the Episcopal Church Foundation in partnership with Forward Movement.

Title 1. Canon 14: Of Parish Vestries

Sec. 1. In every Parish of this Church the number, mode of selection, and term of office of Wardens and Members of the Vestry, with the qualifications of voters, shall be such as the State or Diocesan law may permit or require, and the Wardens and Members of the Vestry selected under such law shall hold office until their successors are selected and have qualified.

Sec. 2. Except as provided by the law of the State or of the Diocese, the Vestry shall be agents and legal representatives of the Parish in all matters concerning its corporate property and the relations of the Parish to its Clergy.

Sec. 3. Unless it conflicts with the law as aforesaid, the Rector, or such other member of the Vestry designated by the Rector, shall preside in all the meetings of the Vestry.

And the rector must . . .

While little is said in the national canons about the roles and responsibilities of the vestry per se, the role and responsibilities of the rector are clearly stated. Title III. Canon 14. Sec. 1 says that the rector is responsible for:

✤ worship and spiritual life;

✤ selection and oversight of all assisting clergy; and

✤ use and control of all buildings and furnishings.

Section 2 of this same canon also spells out the following specific duties of the rector:

✤ education of all ages in the scriptures; the doctrine, discipline and worship of the church; and in the exercise of their ministry;

✤ stewardship education for all ages;

✤ preparing for baptism, confirmation, reception, and reaffirmation;

✤ announcing the bishop's visit with the warden and the vestry, and providing the bishop with information about the congregation's spiritual and temporal state;

✤ applying "open plate" offerings from one Eucharist a month to charitable uses; and

✤ reading communications from the House of Bishops at worship;

✤ recording all baptisms, marriages, confirmations, and burials in the parish register.

In summary, the canons assign virtually all responsibility and necessary authority for the pastoral and spiritual direction of the congregation to the rector. Part of a vestry's "relation to its clergy" is providing the support and intention and resources for carrying out all these responsibilities.

Canons state that when the congregation does not have a rector, the wardens function as the communication link with the diocese; preside at the vestry meetings; make provisions for Sunday worship; are responsible for the administration and maintenance of the congregation's properties; act as custodians of the congregation's registers and records; and convene vestry meetings.   — The Vestry Resource Guide

---

By and large, most of the leadership roles in congregational life, depending on circumstance, training, and individual interest and ability, can, to some degree, be assumed by both clergy and laity. Clergy should seldom be so "otherworldly" that they are totally uninvolved and ignorant of the congregation's temporal matters. Vestries should seldom be so "pragmatic" as to ignore their own pastoral and spiritual development and that of the congregation as a whole. It is clearly not enough for the vestry to provide a place and money and leave the rest to the clergy.

In the final analysis, the rector is the principal and most visible leader of the congregation. The canons make this clear in assigning major responsibility to the rector for the life of the congregation and the use of the buildings.

While the mission of the church is set forth in the Book of Common Prayer, the vestry is responsible for defining the unique mission of the congregation. The congregation, working together with the rector and vestry, is responsible for seeing that the mission is defined, communicated clearly and consistently, reviewed, and updated regularly. A statement of the congregation's mission should:

+ identify its goals;

+ state the populations, communities, or areas they are called to serve;

+ indicate how the goals are to be accomplished; and

+ identify ways for the congregation to recognize progress toward the goals.

The mission statement addresses the questions, "What makes us different? What are our particular gifts and ministries?"

A congregation needs resources to accomplish its mission. The rector and vestry members play a key role in gathering those resources. They must actively give of their time, talent, and treasure if they expect members of the congregation to do so as well. This includes:

✛ participating regularly in worship, as well as in educational and other types of programs;

✛ pledging financial support early in the stewardship campaign;

✛ offering talents to support the congregation's ministry; and being active ministers of the Gospel in daily life and work.

The rector and vestry have the legal and moral responsibility to manage the congregation's resources, including operating funds, investments, furnishings, and buildings and grounds. In addition to its fiduciary responsibilities, the vestry and clergy are responsible for the care of paid and volunteer personnel, insuring that they receive adequate compensation, benefits, equipment, resources, training, and support.

Part of the task for the vestry and the rector is to discern which activities best enable the congregation to fulfill its mission. This includes the development of new programs, events, and services.

Finally, the leadership team needs to reflect periodically on its own work and how well it is meeting its own responsibilities. There is a temptation in the church to assume that everything that goes wrong is the fault of the clergy and lay employees. Yet often the difficulties encountered by the staff are exacerbated by the actions or by the inertia of the vestry. Regular self-assessment through mutual study of ministry can help a rector and vestry address and correct such problems.

FOUR

Spiritual Leadership

As the deer longs for flowing streams,
so my soul longs for you, O God.
— Psalm 42:1

Some say that where angels dwell, demons lurk nearby. The same could be said for any parish, for there are great temptations surrounding those who work in churches — particularly vestry members and clergy.

Gossip can be seductive. "Who pledged and how much? Who didn't pay up this year. Whose fault is it? Why isn't Mrs. Jones in church? Oh, she's angry? At who? Our old rector wouldn't have done it that way, you know. But let's just talk among ourselves . . . " and on and on.

Egos can get in the way. Fatigue can be rampant. Blaming may take place. Relationships may lose vitality. And at the end of the day, the whole congregation may suffer if the vestry and clergy have not kept themselves spiritually centered.

The basics help: church attendance, prayer, Bible study, and the ability to keep confidences. But perhaps what helps more than anything else is a commitment to shared ministry. In walking the path together, the burdens of ministry are lighter, the joys brighter.

The fruits of the Spirit are not gifts that can be earned, for they are freely given by God. But they are available to all who seek them in faith.

Pray for your church. Pray for your vestry. Work at keeping grounded, centered in Christ. And pray that you be open to God's gifts, both known and unknown.

The Spirituality of Authentic Leaders

Bill George

We are all pilgrims, together on a journey through life. On our journey we are searching for our unique way to make a difference in the world. For those of us who believe in God, that search becomes a spiritual journey, tapping into our deeper yearnings to "hear the call" for our lives and to heed that call.

Poet Pablo Neruda spoke to that call in one of his first poems:

> Something ignited in my soul, fever or unremembered wings,
> And I went my own way, deciphering that burning fire.

That fire to decipher the call burns in each of us. But if we go sleepwalking through life, the fire gradually dies out and is eventually extinguished.

When we join with others in pursuing that call, we become fellow pilgrims. In that sense, we are also called to help others and lead them on their journeys.

This is what authentic leaders do. They are true to themselves in pursuing the call as they hear it through their inner voice, yet they are bonded together with others on a similar path.

Discerning our calling

When I was just a teenager, I was strongly influenced by the passage from the Sermon on the Mount where Jesus says, "Let your light so shine before people that they may see your good works and glorify your Father in heaven." I heard it saying to each of us, "We are born with gifts given us by our Creator. Develop those gifts and use them in such a way that they honor your Creator, and that other people will honor him as well, as they see your deeds."

The line between using our gifts to honor our Creator and advancing our own egos is a very thin one.

But how do we discern our calling? What is our purpose in the short span of time that we dwell on this earth? And how do we know when we are following God's call or just pursuing our own ego needs and our self-aggrandizement?

The hardest part of all for me is discerning every day whether I am pursuing God's call or my own ego needs. In the Sermon on the Mount

Jesus admonishes us, "No one can serve two masters.... You cannot serve God and money." In recent years too many of our leaders have ignored or abandoned their calling to pursue the God of money. In doing so, they have abandoned their fellow pilgrims.

The line between using our gifts to honor our Creator and advancing our own egos is a very thin one. I have learned this repeatedly throughout my lifetime. No one can serve two masters.

True north

We are all called to be leaders, each of us in our own way. We are the servants of the people we lead and stewards of the assets of the organizations we are chosen to lead, the most important of which are the human assets.

In becoming leaders, we are called to be the *authentic* person that God created — to be our own person, true to our unique gifts and to our values. Authentic leaders lead with their hearts, with a sense of compassion and passion for those they serve. They establish deep relationships over many years that are characterized by connectedness.

Leadership is not about image, it is not about charisma, and it is not about style.

It is about having a clear sense of purpose for your leadership, based on your calling as you discern it, and practicing your values every day, especially when no one else is looking. To stay true to those values, we must know the "true north" of our moral compass. It is all too easy to rationalize the small steps that give us immediate gratification, yet lead us away from our true north.

This is how so many corporate leaders got in trouble. They didn't start out to do bad things. But little by little, bit by bit, they made marginal decisions that benefited them personally in the short run — winning them praise from their peers and outside observers — yet taking them farther and farther away from their true north. And no one had the courage to tell them they were on the wrong course.

Authentic leaders lead with their hearts, with a sense of compassion and passion for those they serve.

Then one day they realized they were in deep trouble and couldn't hide it any longer. That's when the real trouble began: the gross errors, the defensiveness, the cover-ups, and, ultimately, the destruction of the very enterprise they were responsible for leading.

Staying centered

To avoid these temptations we need to develop practices and relationships to help us stay centered. In addition to regular prayer, I practice meditation twenty minutes twice a day and use exercise like jogging to clear my mind and body of distractions.

But it is my relationships that help me the most in staying centered. In addition to my family, I have the benefit of a men's group where we talk about our lives, our struggles, our dreams, and we pray together.

And over the years my wife, Penny, and I have been part of a marvelous couples' group who come together monthly in a spirit of sharing our beliefs and our lives. Having these groups in our lives is one of our greatest blessings — a gift that helps us stay centered.

Envision yourself at the end of your days with your granddaughter on your knee. Hopefully you will be able to say: "I did my best to use the gifts I received from God to help others. . . . I let my light shine."

Vestry Members as Spiritual Leaders

L. Ann Hallisey

"The spiritual leadership of the parish is the rector's job!"

"I don't know how to talk about it, I wouldn't know what to say."

"Now you're saying we have to worry about being spiritual leaders as well as overseeing the budget, and stewardship, and education, and buildings and grounds?"

These were some of the shocked reactions in a workshop focused on spirituality for vestry members attending a recent diocesan vestry training day. Clearly, they did not see a growing, active prayer life as an essential attribute of vestry leadership. However, quite the opposite is true. Vestry members are indeed spiritual leaders in their parishes. For the vestry is the Body of Christ, and not just in microcosm. In their gathering they represent the fullness of the church — one, holy, catholic, and apostolic. It is the holiness factor under consideration here.

When vestry members individually and collectively take seriously their leadership in the spiritual life of the congregation, their very functioning is influenced. An example: When I was a rector, at our annual mutual ministry reviews, we would ask retiring members to tell us how being on the vestry had influenced them the most. The first time I tried this I expected to hear about the demands on already busy lives or stress on the congregation as our local employer (a naval base) closed its doors.

Imagine the impact on all of us when we heard our most tentative believer say that *her faith had grown* because of being on the vestry, and this is what enabled her to volunteer to run the church school when that position became vacant. The sense of community within the vestry, regular Bible study with which we opened meetings, and the time for silent prayer before a major decision had all deepened her relationship with God.

Sustaining their own spirituality

Vestry members become spiritual leaders by having their own spirituality sustained. What can we offer vestries — large and small — that nurtures and forms their inner lives? How do we transform the agenda of a business meeting into an opportunity for encounter with the living God? How do we nurture our chosen congregational leaders into spiritual role models for the whole congregation?

This does not imply that when one is elected to the vestry one must all of a sudden become a spiritual giant. It does not even suggest that only those with attractive and stellar personalities can assume congregational office. (There are certainly enough cranks and oddities among the saints on the church calendar.) What it means is that one has an authentic relationship with God: a relationship nurtured by prayer, framed by some sort of daily discipline, and anchored by weekly participation in corporate worship.

Vestry members become spiritual leaders by having their own spirituality sustained.

When the vestry gathers to do its work, here are some practical ways to structure the process of getting the inevitable business of the church accomplished in a way that is also attentive to the spiritual life of the vestry:

✚ Mail out the agenda beforehand and invite those who will gather to see the meeting announcement as an invitation to prayer.

✚ Always do some Bible study at the beginning of the meeting, no matter how packed the agenda. Give it just fifteen minutes if you are pressed, but do not ever skip it.

✚ Share a meal or Eucharist, perhaps once a quarter.

✚ Check in: How have I seen, felt, discerned God's presence in my life since the last meeting?

✠ Decision making: Before a decision is made, stop and spend time in silent prayer together.

✠ Make as few yea/nay votes as possible. Instead, utilize consensus.

✠ Sing.

✠ Have a designated "pray-er" during the course of the meeting, someone whose responsibility is not to talk, but simply to be in prayer and in the presence of the vestry, during the meeting. The task can be divided up, with changes made every twenty minutes and an object silently passed from one pray-er to the next.

✠ In closing, talk about: Where have we seen God's presence in this meeting? Where have we blocked God's Spirit in this meeting?

✠ Close with Compline.

✠ Have prayer partners pray for one another in between meetings, and change partners each month. One of my field education students suggested we use colored plastic eggs, with enough for all vestry members, including the rector or vicar. Write one name on each egg. Put them all in a basket and have people choose an egg without looking. Show the eggs when all have chosen one. Partners pray for one another before leaving the premises, and covenant to do so throughout the coming month, until the next meeting. Return the eggs to the basket for next time.

Not all of these suggestions can be implemented, nor should they. However, by choosing some of them you say to one another and to the congregation that you will not tend to the church's business without tending to your own and one another's souls.

Silence in the Vestry:
A Prayer of Opening, of Letting Go
KENNETH ARNOLD

A scene familiar to anyone who has spent more than a few years in a parish goes something like this. The vestry (or any leadership group) gathers for its regular meeting. The atmosphere is tense because everyone knows that "Joe" is going to bring up a controversial issue.

The rector is also tense; she doesn't have the support to turn back Joe's challenge. She begins the meeting with a prayer. Although heads are bowed, everyone is still thinking about the conflict to come. When it comes, it's unpleasant. Joe stomps out in a rage, shouting, "I want my church back!"

I was one of the objects of Joe's anger. I remember being shocked by his vehemence and by his departure. Not too many months after this event, I left the parish. A year later the rector left. Within another year, the congregation had dwindled to a handful on Sundays.

One of the problems with the life of this parish, and I think with many parishes, is that the people did not know how to pray together — although they knew how to gather on Sunday for worship. So how can I say the people did not know how to pray together?

Blessed and cursed

As Episcopalians we are blessed and cursed with a Book of Common Prayer. The book is our refuge and strength; it is also a crutch. Often we feel that having spoken the words in the book, we have prayed. (And often we are right.) What is the difference then between reading the words, or saying the words, and prayer? Does praying together in the spirit — which is different from saying the words of a prayer — make a difference in how we behave with each other in community? How does that work?

In the vestry meeting I described, we were not praying together in the spirit, even though the rector said a prayer and we all bowed our heads. It had already been determined, long before the meeting, that there would be conflict. No one really wanted to pray with the others who were about to oppose what they wanted — no more than they wanted to work out a solution to the problem we all faced. The point of the meeting was to win something over others.

We all face situations like this in our family, work, and church lives. In the secular world, there are all sorts of systems for managing conflict and for helping groups to listen and be respectful of one another. In church, we sometimes use these systems to good effect. But we also have prayer which, if we allow it to use us, can achieve the same results.

Notice I said "allow prayer to use us." Unlike a management technique, which we use properly to achieve a result, with prayer we are asked to empty ourselves to be used: by God. That is what I mean by prayer in the spirit.

Opening and letting go

Ordinarily we think of prayer as a form of asking or seeking. We speak to God, but we also speak to each other. Our prayers are often statements for the benefit of others: Here is my agenda, stay tuned.

The prayer I am suggesting we bring to vestry meetings and other community gatherings is a prayer of opening, of letting go. It is a prayer of

And Jesus said, "I will show you what someone is like who comes to me, hears my words, and acts on them. That one is like a man building a house, who dug deeply and laid the foundation on rock. When a flood rose, the river burst against that house but could not shake it, because it had been well built. But the one who hears and does not act is like a man who built a house on the ground without a foundation. When the river burst... great was the ruin of that house!" —Luke 6:46–49

silence in which no one speaks; everyone listens. The prayer is simply one of inviting God into the silence, into the hearts of all who are gathered. In this prayer, we ask nothing but to recognize that everyone in the room is one being. Everything we do is the work of one organism.

This is the essence of love or compassion: that I see everyone as myself. That is a self-emptying love, not a love designed to achieve an end. To pray in the spirit is to release one's self and let God in the form of everyone in the room come into an open heart.

Could that vestry meeting have ended in some other way had we all begun with this kind of prayer? Probably not, unless we had worked as a community to develop that discipline together. We have to educate ourselves to pray in this way. We have to adopt this prayer as a practice that we incorporate into our daily prayer and into our corporate worship if we are to bring it into the meetings where conflict and dissension and hurt feelings await.

Can we do it?

One way to approach this prayer is for the vestry or any given committee or group to gather on a given occasion and conduct no business at all. I think it is best if the group gathers in the normal meeting room, sits together in silent prayer, inviting God and one another into communion. Everyone leaves at the end of the session, having "done" nothing. It is a test of a community's prayer life: Can we do it?

In a sense this is just a form of meditation in which we try to still the mind. But it is necessary to begin with the intention, perhaps spoken at first to oneself (or even aloud as one simple sentence), to become open to God and to others. It is also useful to be particularly open to the person we most dislike or disagree with. What would have happened that night if Joe and I had opened ourselves to each other in this way, each offering himself to the other?

We might be worshiping together in a vibrant, growing church community.

Discover Your Need for God

Tom Ehrich

It is possible, I suppose, to pray and then to lead. I suggest we try it the other way: attempt the hard work of leading, and thereby discover your need for God.

Leadership of a faith community calls for five spiritual attributes. (Notice that decibels and determination aren't on the list.) Exercising those attributes requires hard work and unconcern for self. Our institutions — not just churches — are starved for leadership because not enough people want to do the work that true leadership requires. They want offices, not duties; they want status, not sleepless nights; they want approval, not conflict; they want control, not accountability.

Reading a prayer from the Prayer Book as a prelude to the vestry's work won't be enough.

True leadership requires more prayers than we are accustomed to saying, more collaboration, more letting go, more listening, more losing, more dying to self — more Jesus, in other words.

I suggest that you start by doing the work, and then when you fall short, struggle for civility, snarl in frustration, and find compromise and consensus unattainable — then, when you have exhausted your own resources, turn to God for help.

Why is it so hard? Leading a church calls for five spiritual attributes that don't come naturally to us.

First, listen

Listen to the questions that people are asking. Listen to their life-questions, not their institution-questions. Listen to their yearnings, frustrations, and brokenness. Listen without intending to fix, or to harvest for political gain, or to assign blame. In the stirrings of the human spirit we will hear God's Spirit.

Second, be honest

It seems quaint and refreshing nowadays when individuals say exactly what they mean to say, intend to do, or did wrong. Normative behavior is to deny, shade, minimize, spin, or simply lie.

When leaders lie, a community's fabric of trust unravels. People make up "facts," guess at reality, lose trust in each other, and become suspicious of outsiders.

Dishonest leaders defend their lies as necessary to protect the institution. Nonsense. The ones being protected are themselves.

Church leaders should set a Godly standard of honesty in all doings, transparency within the community, respect for each other, and trust in God. If we cannot tell the truth to each other, what can we possibly tell the world?

Third, be patient

Leaders need to know the difference between patience and avoidance.

Avoidance looks the other way as problems mount, opportunities arise, people evolve, situations change. Avoidance buys calm today at the expense of tension tomorrow. Avoidance pleases one person today at the expense of failing many people tomorrow. Avoidance loads today's unmet needs onto tomorrow's constituents.

Prodigious efforts to catch up, such as capital campaigns or staff restructuring, often leave the system exhausted, wary, and conflicted.

To exercise Godly patience, leaders must be merciful with human frailty. If people are punished for failure, they will stop trying. If they are scorned for new ideas, they will stop thinking. If they are mocked for aiming high, they will aim low. If only winners get credit, people won't take risks.

Leaders must stay calm when anger erupts — as it will erupt in any institution — and not rush to douse the flames, to take sides, or to exploit anger for personal gain. Leaders must explore what lies behind the anger, allow anger to proceed within healthy bounds, set norms that discourage scapegoating, blaming, and abuse, and work together to affirm open, compassionate resolution.

Leaders must establish an environment of kindness. When people feel loved, trusted, and fairly treated, there is no end to the good they can do. In the absence of kindness, people will be self-protective and grudging in their effort.

Fourth, be tolerant

Religious bullies have declared tolerance weak and intolerance high moral principle. Leaders in all walks of life are having to choose: Will they stand up to religious bullies? Or will they take the expedient course so that business-as-usual can proceed?

This is "gut-check" time for religious leaders. The most basic Christian values are fairness, justice, love, and mercy. When religious leaders can set aside basic values to pursue some church-political issue, the enterprise is lost.

Fifth, see the whole

After Easter, the apostles faced a dilemma. Was their future to be found in the upper room where they were staying, or as Jesus had told them, "in

Jerusalem, in all Judea and Samaria, and to the ends of the earth"? If they took the whole seriously, what was the place of the upper room?

There is work to be done in the upper room, of course, as well as people to know, learning to do, power to receive, healing to mediate, conflicts to be resolved, and joy to be had. One could have a rich religious experience just by staying inside.

Leadership must resist that easy course of staying within the walls, within the known and settled. If the world is changing and people's needs are changing, life inside must change, too. Or else it will become effete, precious, self-serving, and ineffective. People inside must venture beyond the walls. Someone must see larger realities and respond to them.

Personal Reflections on Leadership Challenges

CHARLES E. JENKINS

Rabbi Edwin H. Friedman long ago helped me realize my limited capacity for facilitating change in persons, systems, congregations, and dioceses that are not motivated to change. In a conversation one afternoon Ed Friedman wondered aloud about "the good people of the world who are burning out trying to change the unmotivated."

In my attempts to motivate the Episcopal Diocese of Louisiana not simply to make superficial and perhaps easy adjustments, but to do more and go deeper — to change the way this small, relatively poor diocese relates to the world and to the larger church — I have described the challenge at the level of our "diocesan DNA."

Focusing beyond survival

Shall we, can we, by divine grace change the DNA of the Diocese of Louisiana from that of a declining church very much concerned with ourselves, our survival, and our "issues," to a missionary church focused beyond ourselves?

The first challenge was to convince Episcopalians in Louisiana of the greater risk — in remaining as we were — rather than launching out into the unknown as a missionary diocese. This was not terribly difficult, since by some measures, namely, that of Sunday attendance, we had apparently achieved during the Decade of Evangelism the honor of being the fastest declining diocese in the Episcopal Church!

Money follows mission

To frame the risk we began to describe the potential, in the very least, as "failing forward."

Perhaps the best example of risking "failing forward" has involved the construction of the new Episcopal Chapel of the Holy Comforter to serve the communities of Southern University, New Orleans, and the University of New Orleans. The parish Church of the Holy Comforter was closing. They, and we as a diocese, committed to partner a new collegiate ministry.

To help build the new chapel and fund the ministry to these communities, I called upon one of our leading laypersons in Baton Rouge to ask for a contribution to our capital campaign. He asked, "Bishop, how many Episcopalians do you have at Southern University, New Orleans?" I replied, "None, that I know of. That is the point. We are not here as a chaplain to Episcopalians but as a missionary presence in two university communities." The gent gave a nice gift. Money follows mission.

Walking in grace and trusting God is a spiritual truth into which we continue to grow. An early realization of our need to grow in grace — and God's faithfulness to us — was the attempt to gather our diocesan family together for a Rally Day: a time of worship, prayer, learning, encouragement, sharing, and fellowship.

Only a few registrations

The goal was set that if we could get 750 Episcopalians together in Louisiana we would have done a good work. Many said it couldn't be done. Bishop Michael Marshall was booked to come over from England as our keynote speaker. St. Martin's School was reserved, lunch boxes were ordered, and all the details in place, but few were registered.

Friends and advisors called to urge me to cancel, for this rally was going to be a flop. As my wife, Louise, and I made our way out to suburban New Orleans that day we got caught behind a line of buses. I urged Louise to get past this slow traffic so we could arrive early.

As we began passing the buses I looked up to see faces that I recognized. These were Louisianan Episcopalians making their way to St. Martin's! I don't know exactly how many showed up, perhaps a thousand or so. But most noticeable was the powerful presence of God in that place — a power and an effect far beyond that which I could have made to happen or even planned.

I believe this rally was a good example of God working in this church, and the church walking in and by grace.

From maintenance to mission

The challenges are many, and how this transformation effort shall mature is not as clear to me as I would hope. If the way forward were as

Anchored in the Spirit:
Keeping Grounded

Given the often intense nature of vestry service, how does one stay spiritually grounded? We asked the experts — vestry members, past and present.

✠ "Church attendance was critical. It made a difference to center our vestry meetings in worship as well. We began by checking in with one another and having prayer, lighting a candle to burn during the meeting, finishing with Compline, and sharing a spiritual story. Corporate worship as a vestry and the corporate worship of the parish are *very* important."

— Scott Evenbeck, Indiana

✠ "You have to be there. It was when I was on the vestry, especially as warden, that my whole spiritual life started to develop, for it's in the doing of things that you get involved. Historically, that's one of the reasons for the Daily Office, when you practice your religion "x" number of times a day. In psychological terms, if you want to develop in a certain way you can enter that life through belief, which will lead to practice and then amendment of life. Or you can start with practice, which leads to amendment of life and then belief. Either way, the more you are involved, the more your spiritual life grows."

— Juli Towell, New Jersey

✠ "The type of love I cultivate the most, my primary prayer is 'noticias' — just noticing the people around me and the situation. . . . My attempt to imitate Christ is to start by noticing in the here and now, as he always did: the outcast, the sufferer, the man trying to be out of sight in the tree, the Pharisee, the authority."

— Dick Kurth, North Carolina

clear as I want, little faith would be required to continue the journey from maintenance to mission. But I do have clarity about the triumph of divine love. God who became flesh in the person of Jesus has triumphed over death.

And as we grow into the image and likeness of Christ we find our lives grounded in, and enabled by, that same powerful love which raised Jesus to new life — our joy, our hope, our transformation.

✠ "During my vestry service I found that Bible study, either formal or on my own, helped me keep perspective. It's easy to get lost in the minutia of 'church business.' A warning sign is when vestry service or other lay ministry begins to feel like the day job continued into the evening or the weekend. The wonderful stories of the Hebrew Scriptures or the Jesus of the Gospels are an antidote, and a reminder that what we're about at church isn't just meeting to decide when to have the next meeting." —Dan Austin, New Jersey

✠ "Being called to serve on a vestry asks us to bring our hands-on skills with our desire to serve our parish.... The fact of doing work in fellowship with others in this service creates in us a balance of spirit. Regular worship, especially enhanced by good preaching, music, and liturgy, feeds us. Regular prayer helps us to see the good path we are to follow for our physical, spiritual, and emotional health and 'peace at the last.'" —Lili Whitmer, Connecticut

✠ "Church attendance was more important to me during my vestry service. Since the vestry has a responsibility to the congregation, it is a good place to see the members. While I was on a vestry we had a rector who was found to be using church funds for his personal expenses. I was pretty disillusioned by that episode. But I talked with his replacement and continued to attend church and seemed to retain a spiritual balance." —Greg Young, Minnesota

✠ "We have a small (fifty-plus pledging units) parish so it is important for vestry members, especially wardens, to be everywhere all the time. Services, church school, clean-up days, fellowship events, etc. It's also important to know what is happening in the diocese — whether we are in sync and taking advantage of opportunities to collaborate with other parishes." —Bernard J. Milano, New Jersey

FIVE

Christian Formation

You shall love the Lord your God with all your heart, with all your soul, and with all your might. Keep these words that I am commanding you today in your heart. — Deuteronomy 6:5–6

Will you who witness these vows do all in your power to support these persons in their life in Christ? — from the Baptismal Covenant, The Book of Common Prayer, page 303

Vestry members deal with budgets and finances. And they hire new rectors and greet visitors. They make long-range plans and take care of many details of parish life. But if they are good, and most are, they must also have an unshakeable commitment to opportunities for Christian formation among all parishioners, young and old.

What is Christian formation? As Connecticut writer Sharon Pearson describes her own spiritual upbringing: "I was *formed* by my experiences in a Christian community. Having relationships with adults outside my family, participating in the worshiping community, and sharing my gifts with others were what formed me as a Christian."

More than Christian education, more than study groups, more than youth trips, Christian formation, then, is the range of experiences within the congregation that help shape our souls for Christ.

Christian formation begins with baptism. And we believe it even continues after death, as in the words of the burial office: "Grant that, increasing in knowledge and love of thee, *he* may go from strength to strength in the life of perfect service" (The Book of Common Prayer, page 488).

Strength to strength. From baptism to eternal life. A big responsibility for congregations, and one that vestries need to help inspire. But as with all large commitments, small steps get things going: a handshake, a phone call, an invitation to study the Bible, a special welcome for returning college students, extra help for the church school.

The tools are there. Do your part. It just may make an eternal difference.

CHILDREN

To Exorcise the Ambivalence about Children

Jerome W. Berryman

An exorcism expels by adjuration (to command solemnly or to urge earnestly). It gets rid of something troublesome, menacing, or oppressive. It frees from an evil spirit. I want to exorcise the dangerous ambivalence many adults in the church have about children.

Ambivalence is holding two conflicting feelings at the same time about a person or thing. The word points to a psychological construct, which came into our language from the German *Ambivalenz* via Freud, especially as used in his *Totem and Taboo* (1914). Freud said that the originator of the term was Eugen Bleuler, professor of psychiatry in Zurich. He quipped that Bleuler knew a lot about this, since it dominated his response to Freud's own work.

The views about children in a typical parish range from passionate and single-minded advocacy to an unintended blindness. In general a "practical" bottom line develops. It is that adult concerns come first, because children have no power, no money, no experience, and a lower level of verbal thinking than adults do. All of these observations are largely correct although incomplete.

A false bottom line

The bottom line also recognizes that children are the "church of the future" and that they might bring their parents and other adults to church with them. We, therefore, need to provide something that attracts them, and we need to teach them to be nice, to be quiet, to learn biblical facts, and to be informed about the church. These are not the classical Christian virtues. They are not the beatitudes. Jesus never preached salvation by facts alone. Being nice and being quiet do not serve either children or adults well as prime values. Why can't people get past this bottom line, then?

Both delight and irritation

Ambivalence is the answer. It paralyzes our best thinking about children. It represses both delight and irritation about them. It causes an unconscious acting out of the pain inflicted by holding two opposing feelings at the same time. Deep feelings *for* children stimulate deep feelings *against* children and vice versa, even within the same person. We are caught feeling the need to take responsibility for children and the desire to flee from them for our own freedom.

This oscillating ambivalence needs to be exorcised, because trying to ignore the pain it causes will not heal the distortion.

Integrating childhood and maturity

Jesus understood all of this very well. This is why he integrated childhood in his definition of a well-seasoned maturity.

There are eight primary "chunks" of scripture in the Gospels that show Jesus with children and record what he said about them. Three propositions for a theology of childhood can be developed from them:

1. Our journey of life is like children playing hide and seek. Sometimes God hides. Sometimes we hide. Neither player would play hide and seek with someone who is not there. God is the *Deus Absconditus atque Praesens,* hidden and yet present. This theme integrates the Old and New Testaments as well as childhood and maturity (Luke 7:31–35, Matt. 11:16–19) (John 3:3–8).

2. The silent child teaches by simply being present, for children do not talk about the nonverbal communication systems with which we are born. The child shows us the possibilities of such communication, which we have forgotten because of our reliance on adult language to shape our world. The ontological appreciation of children can reawaken our awareness of body-knowing, which is fundamental to our health and to giving the context for our words. (Matt. 18:1–5, Mark 9:33–37, Luke 9:46–48) (Matt. 18:3, Mark 10:15, Luke 18:17) (Matt. 21:15–16) (Matt. 11:25–26, Luke 10:21)

Almighty God, heavenly Father, you have blessed us with the joy and care of children: Give us calm strength and patient wisdom as we bring them up, that we may teach them to love whatever is just and true and good, following the example of our Savior Jesus Christ. Amen.

—The Book of Common Prayer, page 829

---

3. The relationship between adults and children is so fundamental to the health of both that Jesus shows and tells us about being a blessing to children who in turn bless us by showing God to us by their presence. An ethic of mutual blessing, therefore, is a matter of life and death. This is why Jesus spoke with indignation to the disciples when they tried to keep the children from him. It is why he said that those who cause the

little ones to stumble ought to have millstones tied about their necks and be drowned in the depths of the sea. Horrible as that is, it is better than misleading children about blessing, which can lead to an empty and playless old age instead of wisdom. (Matt. 19:13–15, Mark 10:13–16, Luke 18:15–17) (Matt. 18:6–9, Mark 9:42–48, Luke 17:1–2)

A mutual blessing

To exorcise the ambivalence about children, first, admit in all thinking and dialogue that children need adults and adults need children to be fully human, regardless of one's lifestyle. Children have much to teach us, and we have much to teach them. The ethic of this relationship is mutual blessing.

Second, establish a mutual-blessing "program" in your church. It does not cost anything. It takes no time to organize. The results can be amazing. Whenever you see a child at church get down at the child's eye-level, if you can. If you can't, make a profound bow. Then say slowly, "I'm glad to see you." It will change you, the children, and the church.

If we do this, the larger church can begin to take the lead in discovering and promoting healthy maturity (entering the Kingdom) for adults by mutual blessing. This will help save our species and planet, both of which are endangered. If we don't do this, then it doesn't matter what we do anyway.

Forming Young Christians, Not Just Educating Them

Sharon Ely Pearson

I am a cradle Episcopalian. Sunday school was the place for children, and we worshiped apart from the adults. My memories include coloring pictures, singing "Jesus Loves Me" and "Onward, Christian Soldiers." I received Holy Communion for the first time when I was confirmed at twelve years old in 1967. We wore white gloves and "head doilies," along with our patent-leather shoes. We memorized the Ten Commandments, the Apostles' Creed, and "My Bounden Duty." My "instruction" was complete, and many adults would consider my experience a model to follow.

However, of the twenty-five sixth graders who were confirmed with me, I remember seeing only two of them after confirmation. There was no connection between what we were taught and who we were as Christians.

Today I see some of this same history being replayed in many congregations. Churches are worried about having the right curriculum to teach
in their Sunday schools — for if the curriculum is right, the children will
come, and the church will have a future.

But education is not the answer. It was not for me, it was not for my
children, and it is not for our children now. I was not only educated in
Sunday school — I was *formed* by my experiences in a Christian community. Having relationships with adults outside my family, participating in
the worshiping community, and sharing my gifts with others were what
formed me as a Christian.

Christian Formation. These words are being used more and more in
place of Christian education. And it is the future of our church. Healthiest
and most energized of all are those parishes that view ministries with
children as formational — not just educational. The Christian community
promises to support the newly baptized in their new life in Christ. How?

Participation and practice

Christian formation involves participation and practice. First and foremost, children need to participate in the communal rites of the church.
To see a child's tiny hand reach out for the bread of the Eucharist while
being fed alongside an elder shows children they belong to a community,
not just a family.

Second, all that we see, touch, taste, smell, and hear as well as the
arrangement of space in which we gather influences us. We shape our
space, and it shapes us. Whatever rooms or spaces children gather in for
worship, fellowship, or study, the space (and what is put into it) encourages
or discourages particular actions and interactions. Our environment helps
form us.

Third, the organization of our communal life forms us. By participating
in service opportunities within the parish and in the greater community,
children are able to live out the Gospel, making a connection between
the words of Jesus and our own actions in the world. Life in (and outside)
the congregation should be a sign to the world of what life in God's reign
looks like.

We learn to pray by the practice of prayer; we learn to care for others by
the practice of caring. We learn to respect the dignity of every person by
the way we talk and listen. As Maria Harris states in *Fashion Me a People,*
"the church does not have an educational program; it is an educational
program."

Formation over a lifetime

The Christian education of our children cannot take place in a forty-five-
minute Sunday school lesson. It is learned, experienced, and lived in a

Christian community that views itself as a whole formative process —
taking place over a lifetime. It is continuous. It is integrated. The message of Jesus Christ and God's love and forgiveness will live in the child who experiences the meaning of living out the breaking of bread in a broken world.

Yes, I was educated in the Episcopal Church. But I was also formed, and continue to be so — through the power of the Holy Spirit in arenas of education, worship and living out the Gospel — all of them the bedrock for Christian formation.

Four Things the Vestry Can Do for Your Parish Children

SUZANNE GUTHRIE

As a young Christian I found that a Rule of Life provided a balanced structure in which to grow in love of God and neighbor. These four suggestions form a little Rule vestries can embrace to nurture the children of your parish.

Prayer

Provide tools for children to develop a personal devotional life. *When they enter second grade, give them a Book of Common Prayer.* Encourage them to underline their favorite prayers and psalm lines and to write in the end pages prayers they love that are not in the book, their own written prayers, or lists of sad psalms, pilgrim psalms, penitential psalms. Show them the prayers for preparing for Communion and give them even more — how about using Psalm 84 while they are waiting for church to start? How about Psalm 150 after they come back from communion?

Provide workshops for parents and godparents on prayer, meditation, lectio divina, silence, and observing the liturgical seasons in the home.

Study

Provide a paperback study Bible in the translation you use liturgically for every family in the parish. *Provide a DK Children's Bible (approx. $20) for every family (ideally every child).* * The DK Bible has excellent pictures, maps, artifacts, historical references, and the *story.*

---

*The Children's Illustrated Bible, stories retold by Selina Hastings, illustrated by Eric Thomas and Amy Burch, DK Publishing.

Episcopal liturgy is a feast for the senses, but much of what happens in our worship is lost when we can't bring the chronological story of salvation into the liturgy personally. You might publish in your bulletin not only the lectionary citings for the coming week but corresponding pages in the DK Bible. Why not publish a reading program from Genesis to Revelation that everybody is reading at the same time? When your average six-year-old can cite the qualities of 150 Pokemon characters, you are already missing the deep hunger for community of the biblical family members our children crave.

How can we expect our children to know the Ten Commandments if we do not know them ourselves? Teach them the Commandments, the saints, the doxology; sponsor a contest to learn Bible verses, give them their own Bible and tell them to mark it up.

While many of our schools become more and more like prisons, the church can and should be a place of wonder, mystery, curiosity, learning, imagination, and profound play in the deepest sense. Children are natural theologians. Provide a trip to an observatory. Find a parishioner with a microscope who can show the children brain cells or blood cells and let them wonder aloud at the glory of God. Let your parish be a school of prayer where children can explore divine love with mind and soul and heart. Let them sense that learning in the church is something to grow into — not out of.

Community

Develop a plan to incorporate every baptized child into every aspect of community life. Even a very small child can lovingly polish a chalice. Let your children be on the Altar Guild — teach them the prayers. Let them reverently clean the church alongside adults — listening to sacred music or using meditation techniques complementary to work. Teach them about hospitality and let them help with coffee hour and dinners, ushering, and hosting guests. Teach them the etiquette of talking to everyone at coffee hour and other social skills. I met a child in the Virgin Islands who had a tuxedo from a wedding. When it was his turn to usher, he always wore his tux, to the delight and pride of the parish. Children given mature responsibilities will be mature.

Be sure to follow diocesan guidelines with regard to avoiding situations of potential sexual misconduct.

Mission

Include children in outreach. Encourage participation in the soup kitchen rotation, food pantry, blankets for the homeless, letter-writing. If your church does not have a program of mission and ministry to the wider community and the world, have them participate in another program — Habitat for Humanity, a neighboring church or synagogue program. Be sure to help them bring world and local issues of justice and peace back into their own prayer, study, and intercessions. Perhaps the parish community could have an intercession bulletin board on which there is a map of the world upon which to post newspaper articles, the Anglican cycle of prayer, prayers for peace, pictures and drawings.

You can see the above suggestions form a Rule of Life — from the interior life to exterior service, a plan for growing deeply and widely in Christian practice. Perhaps your vestry can compose an open-ended Rule of Life to live and share in community together.

YOUTH AND YOUNG ADULTS

Youth Minister vs. Youth Ministry

JULIE GRAHAM

Inevitably, the call comes. "Do you have someone, fresh out of college, who could do our youth ministry for us? We can pay for seven hours a week. We'd prefer a male (so we can attract boys to our group), and if he plays the guitar that would be even better."

The dream for every congregation is a sizable youth group with a perky multitalented adult youth leader who is theologically sound and sophisticated. Youth ministry is understood as a Wednesday night meeting of games, songs, and praying teenagers who bring their friends and make plans for the annual ski trip and mission project. The success of youth ministry is measured by how many kids are coming to this Wednesday night gathering.

This is why the call comes seeking that one charismatic person. And this is why the other call comes as well: "Please do not send us more information regarding youth. We do not have enough teenagers coming to our church to have a youth ministry."

Because this is the common understanding of youth ministry, most congregations feel grossly inadequate. For congregations who can't afford to hire staff or don't have needed adult volunteers, there is the belief, born out of a sense of failure, that youth ministry can't exist in their church.

An easy and fun way to involve youth on Sundays: ask four or five of them to read a Bible lesson together, split into parts. Gather them around the lectern, use scripts, and call it "Radio Gospel Theater."

Even those churches who are able to afford the attractive adult youth leader find themselves falling short of realizing the vision of success they have gathered their resources to achieve. Sometimes the kids don't flock to Wednesday night. Sometimes the youth leader leaves after a year, and the kids go too and the church has to start the ministry all over. Sometimes the teens — who were so involved with the Wednesday night youth ministry — after high school graduation are never seen again.

The church asks, "Why are we failing so miserably in youth ministry?" Inevitably, parishioners blame their size, their socioeconomic status, their culture, their neighborhood, their age, or their rector. All along, the fault lies in the vision.

A new vision

It is time for a new vision of youth ministry. "Will you who witness these vows do all in your power to support these persons in their life in Christ?" People: "We will" (The Book of Common Prayer, page 303).

At baptism, the vision is cast of the relationship between the faith community and the newly baptized. The community in all its power is to support this person in his or her life in Christ. The community has pledged to be in relationship in such a way with this person as to increase this person's faith.

Each time this vow is made, the congregation makes itself the youth minister. Youth ministry is the carrying out of the congregation's vow made at its children's baptism.

The most practical model I know for a congregation to organize itself in order to fulfill its baptismal vow is *The Contact Point Model,* published by the Ministries with Young People office at the Episcopal Church Center in New York (1996). This model sees the congregation seeking out and making contact with teenagers at many points in their lives:

✛ Members of the Episcopal Church Women (ECW) write birthday cards for the teenagers associated with the parish.

✠ The parish prayer group divides up a list of teenagers and prays for them on a routine basis.

✠ The adult education team offers regular classes which include "Parenting Teens," "Talking about God and Sex with Your Teenager," and "Praying as a Family."

✠ The outreach committee plans intergenerational opportunities for service in the community.

✠ The liturgy team asks a different group of teenagers each week to lead the congregation in their own version of "the peace." During Holy Week, teenagers are asked to perform their own interpretation of the Passion on Palm Sunday.

✠ The pastoral care committee organizes care packages to be made for the teenagers taking their SATS and for those in college.

✠ The clergy of four small churches organize a joint confirmation program for teenagers, which includes various adults (not parents) as sponsors of the participants in this year of study, search, and service and concludes with a mission trip after confirmation.

✠ A family who owns land in the mountains sponsors a two-week long "family camp" in which all generations live in community and share the cooking, cleaning, and discipline of being together in fun and fellowship.

✠ The hospitality committee organizes a "Friday Night Live" once a month for teens to perform their talents to a live audience of the congregation and community.

✠ The Sunday school teachers and vestry team up to sponsor an after-school program for the children in the housing projects surrounding the church, with the teenagers being trained as the tutors.

✠ The youth advocacy team of another church decides to call each youth (even the ones never seen) every month just to check in.

These are just a few examples of youth ministry that occur when a congregation understands its call to be the youth minister and seeks an integrated relationship with its young people. Youth groups remain part of this vision, but only insofar as they promote that dream of the congregation to support these persons in their life in Christ.

From Spark to Blaze:
Vestries and Vocations

Thomas C. Ely

*At baptism, the congregation promises to do all it can to support
the new Christian in his or her life in Christ. What does that mean
for vestries? We asked Bishop Tom Ely of Vermont to explore how
vestries can make a difference.*

*How can vestries make a difference in helping youth think about their
Christian vocations?*

Our growing understanding of baptismal ministry is a timely incentive for
faith communities and vestries in particular to focus on this challenging
question. The fact that someone would even ask the question is a sign of
health and hope for the church.

In over twenty-five years of youth ministry, I do not recall anyone ever
asking me the question in quite this way. I recall lots of questions about
what vestries can do to help support young people, build stronger youth
programs, and encourage young people to stay connected to the church.
And many individual vestry members have played significant roles in
helping young people think about their vocations. At least half a dozen
such people come to mind in terms of my own life. However, I think this
question is asking something different.

*How can vestries make a difference in helping youth think about their
vocations?*

This is a leadership question, about how vestries might see it as part of
their role and ministry, part of their "agenda," to help young people think
about their future and to think about it in terms of ministry. That is an
exciting prospect! It is a good question for a bishop to ask when meeting
with a vestry and I plan to start asking!

The best way to find an answer is for a vestry to own the question.
Such ownership would send a powerful message of commitment to young
people. It would also send a powerful message about (1) the connection
among baptism, mission and ministry to the whole congregation and
(2) the premise of baptism that ministry in daily life is the primary place
of our human engagement in God's mission.

Vestry members who own this question will more fully share leadership
responsibility for the spiritual lives and journeys of the people they serve.
They will help create and support a community of faith environment in

Keep in Touch with College Students

✛ Contact the campus minister or nearby parish where your student attends.

✛ Share that contact information with departing students.

✛ Send cards or e-mail notes, especially on birthdays or holidays.

✛ Send a care package during exam time.

✛ Get to know students and their interests and then follow up when they return to church during the holidays — e.g., if you know the student is interested in medicine and you're a doctor, go out to lunch.

✛ Invite students to speak to the congregation or youth about college life, its challenges, and faith development.

✛ Offer scholarships.

✛ Send the church bulletin or newsletter regularly — or occasionally with cookies.

✛ Include students on prayer lists.

✛ Provide travel stipends.

✛ Publish news about the students in the parish newsletter.

✛ Invite students to serve in parish ministry and activities.

✛ Explore vocational options with students, including opportunities for ministry.

which the lives, journeys, and questions of young people are listened to, respected, and valued. They will see faith questions in the context of life questions and will model a relational approach to youth ministry, not simply a programmatic approach. And they will affirm young people and their ministries today as well as their ministries tomorrow.

What, then, are some practical ways for a vestry to make a difference in helping youth think about their future?

Pray! Make a point at vestry meetings of praying for young people, their ministries, and their vocational discernment. Include prayers for a myriad of vocations and occupations in the Sunday Prayers of the People and make the "ministry in daily life" connection to those vocations and occupations part of the prayer.

Listen! Find one-on-one, or small group opportunities to listen to young people tell you about what they are doing now and what they hope to be doing in the future. Listen for their dreams, their hopes, their uncertainties, and their fears.

Share! Communicate some of those stories you have heard with others and tell some of your own "vocational" stories to young people. As part of the vestry agenda from time to time, invite members to share with each other something about their own vocations and journeys. Write and encourage others to write about vocational journeys in the parish newsletter or Sunday bulletin. Include young people and young adults away at college among the writers. Find ways (pictures, movies, celebrations) to feature the vocational stories of notable people of faith.

Encourage! Help create a climate in which talking about vocation and career choices is the norm rather than the exception. Help create a climate in which all people (not just youth) talk about their ministries in daily life. Pay attention to, and express interest in, the questions, opportunities, and concerns of young people.

Report! Make "reports from the field" during the Sunday morning liturgy. These are brief offerings of the personal connections between ministry and daily life and work that occur in people's lives. Provide young people and other members of the congregation an opportunity to do this, as well.

Offer! Create opportunities for young people to hear about various occupations, including religious vocations. Try holding Sunday morning "ministry fairs" from time to time featuring members of the congregation and their daily work. Do not forget to include young people and those whose work is centered in the home. Draw on the daily work and vocations of people from all walks of life.

Support! When young people move out of the congregation to pursue further education, or a particular vocational choice, stay connected to them and offer support (moral, spiritual, financial) as a vestry and as a congregation. When they return "home" to the congregation, make a bit of a fuss over them, and continue to show interest and support for their journey.

Don't Confine the Spirit

Lisa Kimball

Vestries, listen carefully. There is a great deal that you can do to strengthen young adult ministry in the Episcopal Church and it doesn't have to cost you a dime. In fact, spending money and building programs may get in the way.

In trying to address the reality that few "young adults" show up in most of our congregations on Sunday mornings, our church has inadvertently displaced incarnational theology with faulty developmental theories. As an institution we have allowed twentieth-century social scientists to convince us that age is a predictor of behavior. First we responded with structures to address the particular and predictable needs of children, then youth, and more recently young adults. We have so fully accepted the recent Western creation of "adolescence" as a universal, hormonally driven stage of development, that we no longer challenge the peculiar assumptions it makes about the maturity of body, mind, or spirit.

What does it mean to be young?

Adolescence (just like our high schools) graduates "young adults" who by default are those human beings stranded somewhere between puberty and full, independent adulthood. In reality, a quick glance across the globe can convince us that "youth" and "young adulthood" are socially constructed phenomena. The expectations and responsibilities of being fifteen or twenty in middle-class suburban North America are different from those that shape the lived experience of the same ages in sub-Saharan Africa. What does it mean to be "young," or to be an "adult," or to be a "young adult"?

Right here in the United States, there are eighteen-year-old married parents serving in the military, nineteen-year-old high school seniors, twenty-year-old city council members, twenty-one-year-old college juniors, twenty-two-year-old bakers, twenty-three-year-old drop-outs, twenty-four-year-old inventors, twenty-five-year-old singles, twenty-six-year-old uncles, twenty-seven-year-old doctors, twenty-eight-year-old musicians, even twenty-nine-year-old grandmothers, and . . . thirty-two-year-old children living in their parents' basements. They are all "young adults." They are all human beings on a life journey.

As Christians, we believe they are made in God's image, and we can see that they are gloriously diverse. The conditions of their lives and the choices they make create ever-changing composites that resist simplistic categories. Although they may not interact with the institutional church

91

as much as we would like, our incarnational theology insists that God-with-us is with them too, whether or not they recognize and name it.

Creative, competent human beings

When the church is able to see beyond the demographic boxes and attendance patterns that have defined young adults, to see them as creative, competent human beings and to notice how God is actually moving in their lives, extraordinary ministry begins. It is ministry rooted in the baptismal covenant. It is mutual. Young adults are encouraged to share their gifts with the church as they experience the personal support and spiritual nurture of our congregations.

What can a vestry do to achieve this?

✤ **Start close to home**. Track down the "young adults" who are active in your congregation and those who grew up in your congregation but may no longer be active. Do not assume that a young adult who no longer attends church has found a new Christian community or has lost all interest in things spiritual. It is more likely that young adults are struggling to balance the demands of their lives and recognize a deep yearning for authentic Christian community. Many stay away from church for practical reasons—work schedule conflicts, transportation, fatigue. Some find our practices dull, irrelevant, or hypocritical, but few have rejected God. Listen to their stories. What is holy? What is broken? What would they welcome from the church? Consider young adults living in the world as missionaries or deacons of your congregation. Love them. Pray for them. Send them care packages. Honor their role as translators and bridge-builders between the institution and the wider community.

✤ **Build on your strengths**. Consider young adult ministry not as a program, but as a pastoral mandate. Rather than isolate young adults, look for opportunities to build relationships across the generations and around common interests. Who in your congregation is best suited to reach out to particular young adults? How might you match individuals who share a common career or vocational interest? How might a young adult's technological skills help an elder in the congregation? What successful event or program could be moved to a time or location that would better suit young adults?

✤ **Trust the unconditional love of God**. There is more than enough love to go around. The goal is not to make young adults conform to the image of older adults, but rather to celebrate the gifts of all ages as full members of the Body of Christ. Let's not make "membership" so exclusive that we confine the Spirit to two antiseptic hours on Sunday morning. Make room for doubt, honor diversity, and invite commitment. Be sure there are snacks!

Young adults are just as human as the rest of us. Young adult ministry will thrive when "they" discover that "we" truly live as if we believe what Jesus taught: that we are worthy, and forgiven by God, regardless of our age.

FAMILIES

Tending the Home Fires

ANNE E. KITCH

One of the most vibrant arenas for Christian formation does not exist anywhere on church grounds. Yet it is an arena that the parish can influence. It is the households of the members.

People who mature in the faith are most influenced by a parent who is faithful. What happens in the home has greater impact than weekly participation in worship or study. *Yet parish leadership often overlooks how to support faith development in the home.*

How might this change? If we are to take the Great Commission seriously — to follow his commandment to teach others "to observe all that I have commanded you" — then we need to be active in our support of families and households and to consider how the gathered community can interface with the household arena.

Ask families to be faithful

Many families with children feel more pressure now than ever about how to devote their time. Sports, arts activities, cultural activities, school bands and clubs all vie for the devotion of families. More and more workplaces demand weekend hours. One parent told me that her son's coach read him the riot act for choosing to attend the parish youth camp during the summer and missing a week of practice. It's hard enough to ask families and youth to choose church over all the other activities that compete for their participation, but when we have to contend with that kind of negative feedback, it seems an impossible task.

But then it's not about competition. And that is the key. We are not asking families to *choose* church among the many activities that our culture offers. We are asking them to be *faithful*. And faithfulness to God is like faithfulness in any relationship. Whether a friend, parent, spouse, colleague, or daughter, to be faithful in our relationship with another requires our presence. We have to show up. We have to communicate our love and demonstrate our care. This is the faithfulness that God requires of us. God is always faithful. God is always present. God continually reaches out to us.

Getting more church into the home

Worship is our loving response to God. Coming to church is coming to God. It is showing up. It is placing ourselves in the divine presence within the community of the faithful. It is good for our souls. As a parish, what we really ask people to do is to extend the loving relationships they share with members of their household to the larger community of the parish. And in return, the parish can honor and nurture household faith.

But how do we do this? I believe it's a matter of shifting our viewpoint. Rather than focusing our energy on how we get more families into church (or families into church more often), the driving question becomes how do we get more church into the home.

One Midwestern church we know is sponsoring Family Bible Scholar Awards. When a child or family completes an entire book of 365 Bible stories, an engraved trophy is presented in church. Kids and parents love it; the cost of the trophy is about $7.50. Sounds like a good investment to us.

By teaching about household faith and providing the skills and resources for people to enact it, we strengthen the relationship between the parish and the home. In God's economy, this inevitably strengthens the entire Body of Christ. It is about the Great Commission, about mission. Taking the message out from the parish into the home. And where do you suppose families that are actively engaged in faith formation in the home will be called to be on Sundays?

Practical steps in the parish budget

✠ Is there financial support in the parish budget for resources that people can use in the home?

✠ Does the parish offer devotional materials for spiritual growth such as Advent or Lenten materials that can be used at home? Are daily devotionals available and easily picked up?

✠ What would it look like if every couple that is married or every family of the newly baptized was given a book of family prayers?

✠ Is there a staff person or a vestry member who is responsible for supporting faith formation in the home?

Practical steps in ministry

Think of your areas of ministry and then intentionally add a component for the household to each.

✠ *Stewardship campaign*

How about making available a children's savings bank? This bank teaches children about stewardship and tithing with three slots for coins: one labeled "store," one labeled "bank," and one labeled "church."

✠ *Evening programs*

Provide parallel programs (e.g., Lenten study) for children, not just babysitting. Thus, when family members return home, they can tell the stories they learned that night.

✠ *Church school curriculum*

Offer activities that families can do at home. What about offering opportunities for families with children of similar ages to get together? Invite speakers in to talk about basic parenting, teenagers and sexuality, or empty nesting.

✠ *Communications*

How about including a regular column in your newsletter with suggestions for family rituals? Or a monthly bulletin notice recommending books, Web sites, and other resources that encourage faith at home.

Accessible and intentional

In the end, we should make sure that our parish programs and meetings are accessible to families with children and provide child care when we want families with young children to attend. In literature, preaching, and teaching, keep the household in mind.

Overall, being attentive as a parish to household faith means being intentional about communicating a concern and love for the home and, in turn, being open and ready for what new call to ministry those faithful households will bring to the congregation.

The Welcome Guest

Caroline Fairless

My bishop once traveled to Papua, New Guinea, and returned with reports of — among other things — what he called edible delicacies, not one of which sounded remotely delicate, or even edible for that matter. He spoke of eating things he had never considered even in his nightmares, because his desire to be a welcome guest in an unfamiliar culture took precedence over his need for comfort.

I begin with this story because it becomes increasingly clear to me that those of us who lead congregations — vestries, educators, clergy, musicians, liturgists, ministers of all kinds — have forgotten, under the guise of hospitality, perhaps, what it means to be a welcome guest in the life of another.

Hospitality suggests that we're the ones at home, and we want to welcome those "out there." But all too often, hospitality turns on the expectation that those to whom we have opened our embrace will soon become as we are. This is particularly true of our liturgy. We say to our prospective new members, "We will teach you how to worship in the right way, namely, the way that we do, and then you can become a participating member of this congregation."

Stepping outside the bounds

To become a welcome guest in the life of another requires that we agree to step outside the bounds of comfort and familiarity, of power and control, to experience what life feels like from the perspective of The Other.

Imagine being a welcome guest in the lives of your teenagers. Imagine being a welcome guest in the life of a family whose children are growing beyond, or who have never participated in, the framework of your cherished patterns of worship. Imagine being a welcome guest in the life of a family new to your church. Imagine being a welcome guest in the lives of all those for whom your rich, familiar, traditional, liturgical, and symbolic life has little or no meaning.

It means going beyond polite conversation to learn something about the ways and traditions, the signs and symbols, the mysteries inherent in lives that are not our own. Being the welcome guest requires that we honor the "stuff" of those lives in ways that allow mutual exchange rather than mere assimilation.

The spiritual lives of children and teens are deep and rich. The spiritual lives of people who have never been in church are deep and rich. The question is not, "How quickly can you become like us?" but rather, "How

Opening the Door

Christian formation for families involves several things, not the least of which is opening the door — literally. Think for a minute. What does the entryway in your church look like? Is it welcoming and free from clutter? That same mind-set is needed when it comes to being intentional about Christian formation for families.

They will need hospitality, worship that embraces them, resources to take home, and opportunities to share in the leadership of the parish sooner rather than later. Most will not fit in the old mold, but that is to the benefit of all, for if given the chance, they will bring both new energies and new ideas.

— Lindsay Hardin Freeman

can you and I together serve as God's creative partners in ways bigger than either of us?"

The discerning of gifts

The adventure lies in the discerning of gifts. What gifts do families, whether or not they are new to the church, bring to the community? And how will your community encourage and support the exercise of these gifts?

The adventure lies in the old and the new agreeing to partner in a new dance, even when the learning of new steps entails many stumbling and bruised feet.

Learning a new dance isn't too difficult, but it does require that vestries and congregational leaders stand together on at least one thing: the belief that a community which is diverse in terms of ecclesiology, experience, age, culture, race, education, economic status, and sexual orientation is a good and desirable thing.

Are you a vestry that gives lip service to diversity? Or are you a vestry committed to developing such a community? It doesn't happen by accident.

It requires that your leadership establish clarity as to how decisions, particularly regarding worship, will be made. Who really makes your decisions? Is it the one who squawks the loudest? Is it the biggest pledger or the old timer? Are your decisions based on personal agenda and personal preference? Are they made by default?

Do the decisions you make honor the full spectrum of your membership? Families, both traditional and nontraditional? The many people who
live at the margins of your congregations? People who are new to your
community? Young people?

If the answer to that question acknowledges room for improvement,
then as a vestry body, undertake the exercises and practices of community building with the help of numerous available resources (see online
www.EpiscopalFoundation.org).

Common congregational practice suggests that we plug people into our
committee structures in an effort to assimilate them into the community.
Recognizing that participation is a good thing, we do our best to match
tasks with human resources.

The conversation often sounds like this:

Q. How do we bring the Watson family more solidly into the community?

A. Well, Bill's had a great deal of investment experience, I understand.
Why don't we invite him onto the Finance Committee?

A. Yeah, and Anita has already told us she bakes for her children's classrooms. What if we ask her to head up the baked goods part of the fund
raising dinner?

A. And isn't the older girl ready for the Youth Group?

But to be a welcome guest means, first, to listen. Maybe Bill will tell
you he wants to serve on the Finance Committee. But maybe he will tell
you that he has a secret love of ceramic sculpture, and that he would like
to work with a few people to design and create several pieces of art for
the sanctuary. You might hear that, if you allow yourself to be a welcome
guest in his life.

Maybe Anita will share with you that the younger of her two daughters
is autistic but has a gift and an appreciation for drama.

A welcome guest in the life of another will likely hear that information.
And once you hear it, you become responsible for it. You hold it tenderly; it
becomes your treasure. And you bring the history and tradition and ways
of your community into the dance with this new thing. You honor the old;
you honor the new, and both come together. Both are changed. Together
you take a step in the direction of a New Jerusalem.

SIX

Stewardship

For where your treasure is, there your heart will be also.
—Luke 12:34

Jesus knew that actions regarding money mirrored the passions of both those who followed him and those who walked away. And that is still true today, for decisions regarding money closely reflect the giver's true values.

In the church, then — at its best — stewardship becomes a year-round approach to understanding time, talent, and treasure. Giving for capital campaigns is cheerful and generous; future generations are blessed with a sound place to worship. Parishioners remember the church as they write their wills and some even endow their pledge. Outreach is an opportunity, not a burden. And even if people are unable to give large sums, 100 percent of all able parishioners make a pledge.

And stewardship at its worst? Low pledging, much grumbling, continual cutbacks, people feeling there are too many "demands" placed upon their money, and clergy feeling they raise money and have time for little else.

Vestries often determine, by their own witness and leadership, the two alternatives above. If the heart of a vestry is sound, parishioners will be inspired and want to be part of the mission and giving of their church. But if not, stewardship can be a very difficult road indeed.

Holy financial and spiritual leadership by the vestry involves setting an example. It means coming to church. It means studying the Bible. It means having a good prayer life and serving others. It means that personal and spiritual priorities are in order. And when those things are in place, the heart of a cheerful giver, vestry member or not, will follow.

Money, God, and Vestries

James A. Kowalski

The church is meant to be that place in history where God's interests for the world meet the interests of the world in the presence of the Holy Spirit. The Holy Spirit seeks to transform a portion of the world into the church so that, as transformed world, the Church may live for the future of the world. — M. Douglas Meeks, *God the Economist*, 23

Money is a great invention. Aren't we better off not having to lug potatoes or chickens (dead or alive) to barter with when we go shopping? Across state and even national borders, we hardly experience any problems because of the confidence people have in money. We give money mythic power, thinking it makes the world go 'round. I personally fear, crave, rail against, and ignore it multiple times each day.

Jesus spoke about money more than any other topic — not counting his overarching message concerning God's reign. And as a priest and citizen, I feel qualified to speak to how we label money — an essentially neutral medium — as the cause of the corruption of individuals and organizations.

So why do we so often hear the complaint, "This parish is always talking about money!" And vestries and clergy worry whether the church isn't becoming "too institutional and no longer religious." Would we be more countercultural if we owned no property and simply focused on spirituality and mission?

Reclaiming stewardship

To struggle with the issues that surround money is a way to reclaim the meaning of being stewards. (How else can we remember that everything belongs to God?) And the danger is that we may fail to continue the dialogue which Jesus spent so much time on — talking openly about money.

The truth is that "movements" come and go unless they institutionalize. For Christ to be "bread for the life of the world," we have to be more than a transient movement; we must institutionalize what we care about for it to survive.

How we do our business can be a significant way to broadcast our integrity regarding faith and the practice of carrying out business in ordinary, commonplace transactions.

The church cannot afford the risk of not doing business well, not only because of possible abuses and malfeasance, but also because we must set an example of how business and values can be integrated in everyday life.

In worship, lifelong learning, and outreach we can set countercultural examples that meet business-like standards: Are we maximizing our resources? Customer-friendly and astute in our marketing strategies? We have a wonderful product to offer — for the life of the world.

The hard choices

Of course there is the wonderful news that money is also portable. Once gathered, we can send it to a neighborhood, or around the world, as we reach out in the name of Christ. And we can transport it across generations and time to amortize costs, and build the kind of shared legacies that make us inheritors of the manifested love of God.

As vestries endeavor publicly to connect faith and the everyday business of the church, we must expect the questions, "Isn't this parish becoming too materialistic? Spending too much on itself?"

I am tempted to think that I was ordained to focus on things other than the business of the church. Yet what credibility would I have if I were not tested by the difficulties of connecting faith to the hard choices of everyday business decisions?

One of my greatest joys, in fact, and a praxis for my transformation as a priest, has been in working with other Christians who happen also to be some of the smartest, most creative entrepreneurs and business leaders I have known.

David Bollier, writing *Aiming Higher for the Business Enterprise Trust* in 1996, told the stories of twenty-five companies. Each prospered by integrating sound management and social vision. Bollier discovered that by "going beyond legal requirements and market place norms, these men and women are determined to bring their personal values and professional lives into closer alignment."

Jesus tells us that he will be present in the bread and wine. Let us open our eyes and ears when he says, "Now, let's see what I can do with the money!"

Enabling Generosity

FRED OSBORN

Members of a vestry are responsible for the church's resources. That usually means obtaining, managing, and directing the use of people, buildings, and investments of and for the church and its ministries.

The daunting task of *obtaining* resources is one which most vestry members abhor. Simply put, people hate asking for money. Yet someone must do it!

For years churches have shunned the more "secular" approaches to fund-raising that prove so successful for colleges, museums, hospitals, and other charities ("Here at St. John's, we don't do fund-raising; we do stewardship!") as if "fund-raising" were somehow tainted, dirty, or sinful. Yet the frequent abuse of the word "stewardship" has tainted it to mean, simply, fund-raising.

A bishop for whom I worked some time ago announced to a parish he was visiting, "Your stewardship is up!" Did he mean that the people of this parish were living more responsible lives, seeing the world, their skills, and talents as gifts from God, acting out of a sense of abundance with generosity? No. He meant that the parish's pledge income was up. Is that what stewardship has come to mean?

A sacred spiritual context

As vestry members, we must take our responsibilities to obtain resources seriously; we must do so in a sacred, spiritual context, but we must also understand how other, more secular charities raise money. There is much for us to learn from them.

At the Foundation's new Academy for Episcopal Philanthropy we are teaching a new approach that melds together the two approaches — sacred and secular.

In the "sacred" approach, we talk about life as a blessing, as a gift from God. When we see our lives as gifts of God, we can respond with gratitude. As we get more and more into that gratitude, we discover that the extent of those blessings is not only sufficient for our needs, but also overflowingly excessive! This recognition of abundance in our lives is, to me, the core "good news" of the Gospel. Once we see the abundance of the gifts we've been given, we can be free of the sense of scarcity with which the market economy bombards us day in and day out.

How splendid to be able to say, "I have enough!" How magnificent to be able to say "I choose not to do this or that with my money" instead of saying, "I can't afford it."

Of course, seeing such abundance in our lives is not practical. It is not realistic. It is not prudent. It is magical, mysterious, and built on the sometimes shaky foundations of faith.

Just as our "sacred" approach has four elements — gift, gratitude, abundance, and generosity — the "secular" approach, too, has four elements:

✠ DO something worthwhile and tell the story about it

✠ ENGAGE people who might be interested in that kind of work

✠ ASK them to give money

✠ THANK them over and over again

Colleges, museums, and hospitals do an excellent job of "making the case," telling you what they're doing with the money you sent them, and telling what they might do if you send them more. Church people need to be less reticent to "show off" the good works they do. If people don't know about them, how can they help support them?

Say thank you

It is also important to connect the people to the good work that their money has accomplished. Say thank you by telling people the story of what your church is able to do because they gave it money.

Engaging people is a long-term process that brings them from awareness, through knowledge, caring, and commitment, to a sense of involvement sufficient to make them comfortable with investment. They know your church well enough that they'll entrust their money to you because they know you'll use it wisely and well.

Asking for money is usually done in two ways: in person and in print. In person, solicitation usually means visits, sermons, seminars, and telephone calls. Print methods, through articles in the parish newsletter about what good things the parish has done are also effective.

And finally, thanking. So many churches could be better at making people feel that their contributions are important and appreciated. Remember, the best motivation for giving is a good experience of giving.

Feel comfortable with your own attitude toward the gifts God has given you. Understand the relationship you have with your own money. Knowing some of the concepts that we teach to meld the sacred and the secular should make you more comfortable with your vestry role as one who obtains resources for mission and ministry.

For more information about the Episcopal Church Foundation's Gift Planning programs, contact the Foundation at (800) 697–2858 or see online *www.EpiscopalFoundation.org.*

Thoughtful Stewardship Beyond the Tithe

CALEB LORING III

"All things come of thee, O Lord, and of thine own have we given thee" is a familiar phrase to most of us, spoken as our church offerings are brought before the Lord. It's such a simple, yet profound, phrase that lifts our eyes from our wallets to the horizon of life itself, to behold the full aspect of our present being — time, talent, treasure.

Two incidents in my life drove this phrase home to me. The first happened twenty years ago, when I was a younger married man with two children. My wife and I had raised our level of giving to 6 percent of our pretax income. Feeling pretty smug about this, I went to a Christian breakfast group in the area to hear a prominent local Christian businessman address us on the concept of giving. He noted that *all* we have comes from the Lord, and that we owe it *all* back to him. He shared with us that he had moved beyond the concept of the 10 percent tithe to giving away over 40 percent of his pretax income, a level that had been audited more than once by the Internal Revenue Service.

As a footnote, he added that he felt he could give more. What a challenge this was to all of us there, and from a member of the local Episcopal Church as well!

The second incident happened three years ago. Because of the recent economic strength and growth in financial assets, which have accrued to the benefit of a number of people, the chairman of the board of Gordon-Conwell Theological Seminary (on whose board I serve) challenged the board to consider a one-time tithe on their assets (i.e., give away 10 percent of assets) to help the seminary with its capital campaign. This challenging thought has led me to be more generous in capital giving over the last three years.

How does one reach a point of deciding or being open to the concept of what *"All* things come of thee..." means in terms of our life? First, over time, we must truly embrace the meaning of Christ's sacrifice for us: we were bought for a terrible, horrific price that truly demands our *all* in response. As we have come to know Jesus, to love him, and to truly want to serve him, the Holy Spirit teaches us how to give our *all* back in response. This process of knowing, loving, and giving is a life-long exercise and one of continuing challenges that leads to growth.

In addition to and through study and prayer, we learn in community, as is evidenced by the two incidents outlined above. This leads me to observe our need to have a healthy community at our church. A study was performed by Vision New England (a.k.a. The Evangelistic Association of New England), where I serve as chairman of the board. The results were captured in a book entitled *Becoming a Healthy Church: Ten Characteristics* by the Reverend Stephen A. Macchia.* These characteristics of a church community are as follows:

---

*Stephen A. Macchia, *Becoming a Healthy Church: Ten Characteristics* (Grand Rapids, Mich.: Baker Books, 1999).

1. God's Empowering Presence
2. God-Exalting Worship
3. Spiritual Disciplines
4. Learning and Growing in Community
5. A Commitment to Loving/Caring Relationships
6. Servant-Leadership Development
7. An Outward Focus
8. Wise Administration and Accountability
9. Networking with the Regional Church
10. Stewardship and Generosity

These characteristics are listed in the rank order resulting from surveys described in Macchia's book. In sum, your church and your relationship with God, including spiritual disciplines, need to be in order (1–3) so that you can function as a healthy person and church community (4–6) and to go out into the world in a wise and accountable fashion (7–10) with generosity.

How are you and your church doing with regard to these characteristics? These attributes certainly encompass the *all* of what comes from God and the giving of *all* back to him.

Finances: Leading by Example

BILL NOLAN

Like pruning a vineyard in a drought, how a parish spends its money during tough times is critical — and like it or not, sends a strong message to parishioners about their own spending.

Outreach: fixed or variable?

Many years ago I served as a commercial loan officer for a major bank. My area of expertise was lending money to churches.

As bankers, we did not want to ever foreclose on a church. We had to be completely confident that the cash flow was available to pay back the loan.

When we analyzed the profit and loss statement of a church to find the source of repayment, we always heard the same story: "If money ever gets tight, we can always divert the allocation for missions and outreach to debt service." Missions and outreach was often a rainy day account that could be used elsewhere, as circumstances warranted.

Tough times

The last two or three years have been tough on stewardship. Major economic indicators are down, personal income is stagnant, and the boom years of the 1990s are long over. *If your annual stewardship is suffering, are you tempted to reach into the line item entitled "missions" in order to meet other expenses?* Isn't it more important to keep the church doors open than it is to send money to Africa or somewhere else? Someone else will do that. Besides, it is only for a year or two....

Completed parochial reports for 2004 (7200 Episcopal congregations) indicate the median investment portfolio for Episcopal churches is $126,109 (among churches that report investments); the median total revenue is $152,367; the median total expense is $154,045, and the median operating expense is $134,617. Source: C. Kirk Hadaway, director of research, the Episcopal Church Center.

Consider this analogy. Families in your congregation have income and expenses, just like your parish. Some of those expenses are fixed and some are variable, just like your parish. Normally it is easier to control expenses rather than raise revenue, just like your parish. What expenses can be controlled? Ah, perhaps the family tithe. Isn't it more important to pay bills than it is to send money to the church? Someone else will do that, right? Besides, it is only for a year or two....

Sending the wrong message

When a vestry decides to cut or reduce its outreach budget in order to meet the normal operating expenses of a parish, it sends a message to parishioners: the tithe is variable, and is dependent upon circumstances. If times are tough, it is acceptable to reduce or eliminate what you give to God until things get better. As leaders, is that the message you want to send?

As a vestry, your parish tithe is basically what you decide to allocate to missions and outreach. It is no different than what a family allocates to charity. Obviously a family's annual pledge will be controlled somewhat by its annual income, but it should never be considered an expense that can be eliminated as needed. If one's car payment goes up by $150 a month,

> *Leading by example: Shoe repair shop owner Bob Fischer of Wayzata, Minnesota, sleeps outside through rain and snow beginning in mid-November each year until the local food shelf has reached its fund-raising goal. Over the past eight years, Bob has helped raise some $3 million. He's usually in his tent for about a month, and in Minnesota, it gets pretty chilly.*

does that mean the tithe should go down by that much? The pledge should be impacted by income, not by expense.

Consider these averages

According to the Faith Communities Today study (*http://fact.hartsem.edu/denom/denom-frame.htm*) the average Episcopal parish spends its money as follows:

Staff salaries/benefits	46.0%
Operating expenses	23.0%
Episcopal mission work	10.7%
Capital improvements	6.7%
Program support	5.5%
Other mission work	3.6%
Reserve or investments	2.0%
Other	2.5%
TOTAL	100.0%

How do your parish expenses compare? Of those expenses, which ones are variable and which are fixed? Without getting into deep cuts, assume that "salaries and operating expenses" are fixed. That comprises 69 percent of your annual income. What of the remaining 31 percent is variable?

Missions work is almost half of what is remaining. It is easy to see why it is so tempting. Programs and capital improvements are for the members, whereas missions and outreach are for everyone else. Don't we need to care for our members first? Again, bring this down to the family level. Is a new television or couch or room addition a capital improvement for the family? Should that impact the tithe?

It can be a blessing

Tough economic times can be a blessing to a parish. When times are great, we often become reckless with what we support. Programs are funded without any accountability, and ministries are funded without a clear sense of whether it corresponds with our parish mission or vision.

Money actually allocated to missions doesn't always square with what's written in a parish's mission statement. The Faith Communities Today study found that "83% of Episcopal parishes have articulated their purpose and direction in a mission or vision statement. However, this same mission statement is only used to determine spending priorities in 13% to 26% of the parishes surveyed."

In tough times you have the opportunity to review programs and specific missions you support to see if they align with your mission statement. If they do, keep them. If they don't, consider them fair game.

Authentic Tough Talk: Tight Times, Hard Decisions

DICK KURTH

Who would disagree that authentic, honest talk about money is one of the very toughest things a vestry has to do? It is particularly hard in tough economic times, when it is most necessary.

Every time we present a budget to the community, we are asking for something. How, then, to communicate in such a way that people believe what we are saying? Whatever the hard choices we have made — to maintain one program at the expense of another, to defer badly needed repairs, to lay off staff, or even to run a deficit — have been made after much debate and prayer and in good faith. Will the community support us?

Believing it ourselves

The first thing we need to be sure of is that we have actually done all of those hard things we think we have done. In other words, to be believed we must believe it ourselves.

A few years back our vestry went through a discernment process exploring who we were and who we wanted to be. This followed a period in the early 1990s when recession, clergy turnover, interim ministry, less than crystal clear accounting, deficits, and staff layoffs led to real pain and distrust in the parish. To help heal, a vestry pledge had been made to balance the books every year come what may. There would be no surprises. That promise was kept. After six or seven years of stability, we sensed that trust had been restored. Now it was time to dream a little. Things felt good in the parish. We were ready for the next level.

Under the leadership of three very capable senior wardens over two years, dream we did: What would the church look like if we glorify God in a way commensurate with our underlying resources? Moreover, what if we went beyond the basics and were able to raise whatever funds we needed? We took our time; there was real depth and enthusiasm. After costing our dreams, we came up with an annual budget roughly $300,000 at a minimum and $500,000 at a maximum over where we were (approximately $900,000 total).

Successive treasurers wanted to hustle through the routine; other members did not want to look stupid.

By and by stewardship season arrived. The senior warden asked all vestry members to significantly increase their own pledges in order to lead the parish in this fresh beginning. Our vestry goal was an increase of 33 percent over a couple of years.

As I remember it, pledges from the vestry went up a paltry 2 percent.

I was junior warden at the time, shortly to be senior warden. I was terrified. I knew that this vestry really wanted the things it had dreamed. I knew that times were relatively good. I knew that the parish was not on the warpath.

The rector and I started asking each other questions. What was it we didn't know about ourselves? Our tradition is to find our treasurer, stewardship, and finance committee chairs from among the bankers, traders, and investment managers in our community. They had, over the years, done a great job of ensuring that we stayed within our limits. But, we asked ourselves, what do our budget discussions feel like? Not particularly good. We know what is said, but what is the relational tone? Maybe the nonfinancial people running programs were intimidated?

Not trusting the budget

We developed a hunch that there wasn't a collective understanding of the budget we already had. Not trusting the budget, the vestry was not equipped to field questions from the parish about it.

Rarely were there any serious financial questions at vestry meetings and when there were, the answers were often defensive. Successive treasurers wanted to hustle through the routine; other members did not want to look stupid. And of course, things were in good shape. We hadn't run a deficit in years. We were stuck without being aware that we were stuck.

We pushed and pried in private with some vestry members. What were their real attitudes toward "the numbers"? We learned that there was a widespread assumption that there was a lot of slush in the budget, only that it was going to some program other than their own.

We scheduled a series of non-mandatory meetings over the summer to completely and thoroughly shine light on the budget. A lot of work went into these; no question was too small, and, frankly, no question was too dumb. Since it put the responsibility and the opportunity on each of us personally, every vestry member came to every meeting. We had a lot of fun. When we were finished, we had an absolutely solid foundational budget, and we proved what we had been saying all along. There was no slack at all in the budget, only now we knew that for certain. Our treasurer was vindicated. But now he knew how to talk a community talk. He knew that people were with him step by step.

Maybe best of all, we eliminated a lot of tangential conversation that was really about money, but didn't come right out and say so. And the vestry's own pledges went up — from 2 percent to 36 percent!

Authenticity flows from knowledge and belief. It creates genuine movement and unsticks the stuck. We should always question our assumptions to be sure to learn what we don't know. And like all true knowledge, we come by it personally, firsthand. Don't we owe that to ourselves and to the communities we lead?

SEVEN

Planned Giving

Do not store up for yourselves treasures on earth, where moth and rust consume, and where thieves break in and steal, but store up for yourselves treasures in heaven. — Matthew 6:19

Asking people to leave the church in their wills or estate plan has always been a tough task for clergy and vestries. But here's the bottom line: congregations have nothing to apologize for when asking parishioners to consider leaving the church in their wills. On the contrary, experts within the church say that people respond positively to regular and sustained conversations about planned giving. Opportunities for estate planning, living wills, and funeral wishes must be available, or else the church will not have done its part to help parishioners ensure that their wishes upon death truly reflect their values.

An added reason for thinking about planned giving is that some $41 trillion will pass from one generation to another by 2052, according to the Association for American Retired People (AARP). Museums, schools, parks, and other organizations continually approach people for contributions; the church should do no less.

So how to best go about encouraging parishioners to leave money to the church through their wills or estate plans? Two approaches: (1) say nothing and generally hope people will be generous, or (2) believe that fellow church members do want information and opportunities that will help them think through their final plans in a Christian context.

How can vestry members be a part of such an important step? Perhaps the best place to start is in thinking through these issues yourself:

✠ What really matters to you as you consider the future?

✠ What about your pledge; is there a way to endow it?

✠ What kind of legacy, small or large, might you leave for future generations in the church?

✠ If you were not able to tithe in life, is there a way to do it in death?

Once you have taken steps to put your own plans in order, it will be easier to encourage a faithful response from others. Start a legacy society. Provide routine opportunities. Suggest sermons about planned giving. And know that a first step is better than none at all.

Ready to Receive

CHARLES GEARING

When John and Sarah Coleman wrote their will, they wanted to leave a substantial amount — around $1 million — to their much beloved parish. But then came a key question from their attorney: "Do you feel comfortable with the way the church might handle a gift of that magnitude?"

After thinking about it, they were not confident that church leaders would manage such a gift in a careful, prudent way. They worried that the funds might be dissipated quickly, not leaving any significant footprints in the parish history. Unfortunately, the Colemans made other arrangements.

This is not a far-fetched scenario, and it could apply to many, if not most, parishes at some time in their lifespan. How might you make preparations so that a prospective donor will feel confident about your parish's ability to exercise good stewardship of a major gift? Put in place a well-woven basket of structure, awareness, and response.

Structure

A sound structure — permanent, competent, reliable, accountable, and responsive to donors — assures benefactors that gifts will be managed well and that the church will be faithful to any restrictions or limitations the donor stipulates, in perpetuity. To set it up, you will need a formation resolution by your vestry that creates an endowment fund and provides for its management, usually in the form of a separate board, with by-laws. With a clear vision, the resolution should define how the endowment will support the parish's ministries and mission.

Addressing these questions is also helpful:

✠ By what means do funds get into the endowment? (For example, are all monies the parish receives by bequest directed automatically to the fund?)

✠ Are designated or restricted funds welcome? Is there a minimum amount that is required to maintain a separate, designated fund?

✠ How will the investment function be managed?

✠ How do funds get out of the endowment fund — i.e., what are the spending rules to determine how much is available for expenditure each year?

Awareness

After the structure is in place, consider how you might motivate parish-ioners to make provision for the church in their estate plans. You need to be intentional, creative, steady — and patient. It has been said that *"Procrastination* is the most formidable enemy of planned giving." I can assure you that your experiences will tend to confirm this. You just have to stay at it.

You may want to create a legacy society, which can aid in the educa-tion/awareness program. Preparing a descriptive leaflet and conducting an information program is inherently more interesting to parishioners under the aegis of a legacy society than simply talking about "planned giving."

The rubric on page 445 of the Book of Common Prayer is especially helpful:

> *The Minister of the Congregation is directed to instruct the people, from time to time, about the duty of Christian parents to make pru-dent provision for the well-being of their families, and of all persons to make wills, while they are in health, arranging for the disposal of their temporal goods, not neglecting, if they are able, to leave bequests for religious and charitable uses.*

Given its priority of putting families first, this rubric helps establish the "tone" of the planned giving effort, for making arrangements for the dis-position of one's worldly goods is inherently a *pastoral* issue, not a church fund-raising event. Begin the program with a letter to the congregation from the chief pastor, the rector.

Design your funeral service before making out your will. The funeral can then be a reflection of your life, a message to loved ones about what was important to you. Then write or amend your will so that it reflects those values.

Once this has taken place, there is no end to the possibilities for con-tinuing to make your parishioners aware of opportunities to complete arrangements for their final affairs and provide for the church in their es-tate plans. Most parishes use the parish newsletter and service bulletins for articles, inserts, notices, and regular "one-liners" (e.g., "The spirit is willing, but where's the will?")

Periodic mailings can be directed to a specific demographic group, such as those fifty-five and over, and special events, such as a "wills clinic" or a "final affairs fair" can be held. All of these provide time and motivation to discuss the role of Christian charitable giving in estate planning.

Approaching the awareness task as part of the overall stewardship education program is key, for the stewardship of accumulated assets is the logical next step.

Many of us strive to tithe during our lifetime but are unable to reach that goal. I have known a number of Episcopalians who found comfort in allocating 10 percent of their estate to their church, thus completing a personal goal in death, if not in life.

Response

"*If a parishioner shows interest in making a planned gift, how do we best respond?*" Before anyone asks for help, it is essential to work out the answer to that question.

First, identify the key contact person, so that when a question is raised, every parish leader is prepared to make an unequivocal reference. Your contact person is the one who knows enough to be comfortable in a first conversation with the prospective donor and can easily access additional resources.

The Episcopal Church Foundation, with the responsibility for the planned giving ministry in the Episcopal Church, is the principal resource for assistance and support of parishes in their planned giving programs. Parish representatives should feel free to call the Foundation office for assistance or information, (800) 697-2858, or see online *www.EpiscopalFoundation.org.*

Only If We Ask

FRED OSBORN

Wilma, eighty years old, wasn't feeling very well when she got dressed one chilly Sunday morning and went to church.

Even so, she was thrilled to hear the rector report that Gladys, a good friend of hers, who'd died just a few months earlier, had left a bequest to the parish.

Wilma said to herself, "I'm going to do the same thing! I love this church, and I want it to thrive so my friends and neighbors — and their children — can enjoy it. After all, I'm not taking my money with me!" On her way out, she spoke to the rector quickly at the back of the church, telling him she was anxious to do something for the church "like Gladys did."

Wilma promised herself that she'd call her lawyer the next morning and arrange something. But on Monday morning, Wilma felt worse. That afternoon she went into the hospital.

Her rector came to see her on Tuesday and she told him that the doctor reported rapidly spreading cancer — but that she'd lived a long life and was ready to die when the Lord was ready to take her. She and the rector prayed together. The rector said nothing about Wilma's words that Sunday; he felt it was a bad time to sound like he was asking for money.

Wilma died that Friday; her will was read a week later. With no heirs, her estate, to the community's surprise, exceeded $500,000. Her will left the bulk of that money to her college, from which she'd graduated some sixty years earlier and to which she'd not been back since. There was no provision for her beloved church.

Wilma is not alone. With some $50 trillion changing hands as Wilma's generation passes on, there are many instances in which well-meaning, generous people make bequests. They will leave assets to their beloved churches — but usually, only if churches ask.

Important learnings

The church in this story, St. Matthew's, learned two things. The vestry learned the importance of a legacy society (see the following article), and all members of the vestry now belong.

Develop a mind-set within your parish where it is acceptable to talk about death, dying, and planned giving, and offer opportunities for such reflection routinely.

Wilma's rector realized he has a pastoral duty to help people who are facing the end, on their "deathbed," as it were, to reflect on Christian teachings about death. He was right that such a time is not a good time to ask for money; but it is a good time to help people insure that their estate plans reflect their values.

Money left wisely... or not

The Episcopal Church Foundation hears stories like Wilma's frequently, about money that is left wisely and money that is not, wills made or not made at all, or wills left in some form that was good twenty years ago, but irrelevant to the situation when the person dies. It is heartbreaking when good intentions are not put into action because the instructions were never given.

How can you help parishioners to reflect their values in their estate plans? Develop a mind-set within your parish where it is acceptable to talk about death, dying, and planned giving, and offer opportunities for such reflection routinely. Point out what others have done. Most of all, take immediate action to be sure that your estate plans express your values. We don't know when we'll go, but we do know we're not taking it with us.

Securing the Future:
The Promise of Legacy Societies
Lindsay Hardin Freeman

At many parishes, Memorial Day weekend is a time of empty pews and thoughts of summer. But at Emmanuel Episcopal Church on Mercer Island, just east of Seattle, the Sunday service begins in the church's memorial garden, with prayers for those buried there. Then, following a bagpiper inside, parishioners hear a sermon that encourages them to remember God's work and sacred places in their wills.

According to Glenn Ledbetter, a local realtor and chair of Emmanuel's endowment board, the goal is to raise the current endowment from $250,000 to $2 million. As an incentive, those who sign up this spring will be known as founding members, and will have their names on a first plaque in the narthex.

For Ledbetter, it's all about the future. "The whole message is about what one generation is going to give to the next generation," he says. "If you don't have something that's worthy of the marketplace, you deserve to go out of business. But if you believe in your church having something to offer future generations, then you need to help that happen."

Not one negative voice

Some parishes, like Emmanuel, use legacy societies to increase the endowment; others, like St. Paul's by the Sea in Jacksonville, Florida, are creating an endowment through bequests.

"Our parish has never had an endowment," says Tony Gabrielle, a retired executive and chair of the endowment board at St. Paul's. "We haven't been in a position to feed new ministries that come up periodically — so we are changing that."

St. Paul's goal is to enroll half of its ninety-six families in its new "Tree of Life" legacy society for an initial endowment of $250,000.

Some fifty families have been contacted to date: the response has been overwhelmingly positive.

"Out of all that, not one negative voice," says Gabrielle. "As this thing gathers publicity and momentum, I really think it will work."

Sustaining the momentum

Such momentum is key when setting up a legacy society, says Charles Gearing, a national expert in the process and recently retired director of diocesan programs at the Episcopal Church Foundation. The problem comes, he says, if that momentum is not sustained from year to year. "Planned giving is unique in that there is a substantial time lag between when a person makes a decision to give a gift and when that gift is received," he says. "The challenge is to keep people feeling good about their commitment within that time frame."

Consistent communication, including regular events and periodic mailings, Gearing says, helps keep that energy going.

For it is in giving that we receive and it is in dying that we are born to eternal life. — St. Francis of Assisi

---

Such events might include an annual dinner with an outside speaker focusing on issues of life and death, legacy and remembrance, generosity and abundance. Names of legacy society members are often posted on a plaque or engraved on a sculpture, and members should receive one or two special communications a year, updating them on ministries made possible because of bequests.

Does the work pay off? Gearing says yes, unequivocally. "The more we live with this task of planned giving in the church, the more important it becomes. It's just confirmed over and over again. It's indispensable."

When the Nest Egg Shrinks

FRED OSBORN

People die. They don't take anything with them. They leave everything they own behind. Through their estate plans (if they have any), they give what they own to other people, the government, charity — and hopefully their churches.

The Top Ten Myths about Gift Planning

✠ Gift planning is only for the rich.

✠ Gift planning lowers annual stewardship.

✠ Gift planning is too complicated.

✠ I don't have enough assets to make a will.

✠ This can't be important because it's so boring.

✠ The church doesn't know what to do with my money.

✠ Younger people don't need wills.

✠ No one wants to talk about death.

✠ Clergy can't talk about money.

✠ Church people don't need to be thanked.

Since Episcopal churches have existed in the United States, endowments have been created by generous people who have left property and money through bequests.

How should those endowments be used? Should parishes have an endowment at all? How should they be managed? *And how do you manage your parish's operations when the value of the endowment shrinks?*

Using endowments

The way endowments are used is often predetermined by the donor and generally supports five categories of church life: building maintenance, Christian education, music, youth, and outreach/mission work. Exciting, creative uses of endowments in these categories enhance outreach and service.

Sometimes endowments are used in less exciting ways, like supporting the church's operating budget. If that is the case, a certain complacency often becomes ingrained in the vestry and clergy, for relying on the income from dead people's money can yield a dead church. I know of one parish where the endowment income is sufficient to pay the clergy, maintain the building, and pay a full choir. They don't even need a congregation! And they do virtually nothing beyond their buildings and music (which are lovely, by the way).

Should you have an endowment?

How an endowment is used is at the heart of this question. If everyone would tithe, we wouldn't need endowments. Perhaps so. But everyone doesn't tithe, and endowments can be a strong force for mission.

Here at the Episcopal Church Foundation, *we believe that parishes of all sizes, small and large,* should have endowments and that they should be used in ways that support the mission of the parish.

Managing endowments

Vestries, because they are responsible for all material assets of the parish, are responsible for receiving, managing, and using endowments. In larger churches this responsibility is often delegated to a finance or investment committee. Vision, policies, and marketing need to be tight, focused, and in writing:

+ **Vision:** What is your vision of how endowment funds will be used? Is it available to potential donors? Trouble arises when this vision in unclear or nonexistent.

+ **Policies:** Potential donors want clear policies to assure them the money will be managed well and for the purpose they have stipulated. Guidelines should address the kinds of gifts that are acceptable (types of assets, minimum size); how the funds will be managed (investment policies, risk tolerance, asset allocation, total return expectations); and how the funds will be used (spending rules or how much "draw down" is authorized).

+ **Marketing:** Engage and educate. Get the word out about long-term gift planning. Help parishioners understand the benefits for both congregation and donor.

Dealing with shrinking assets

Many churches use the total return method of calculating how much they will draw from their endowment each year. They measure performance by adding together capital growth and income, and draw down a consistent percentage of the total asset value each year. Some use 5 percent based on a three-year rolling average of asset value.

For those who calculate their draw down on a rolling average, the impact of a bear market is softened, or "smoothed," and its effect on income should be minimal.

Those suffering from more severe drops in income should consider changing the formula temporarily. After all, endowments are often considered insurance for a rainy day, and the investment markets have had pretty crummy weather in the last three years! Reduce activity, fire staff, and close down programs only as a last resort.

Fred Osborn

Indeed, abundance and scarcity issues are in sharp relief when our net worth falls. Relative wealth comes to me with a bang when I'm reminded that 60 percent of the world's population has never made a phone call!

And relative wealth from a parish perspective comes clear when I'm reminded that more than half of Episcopal churches have annual budgets less than $100,000.

Get creative

If possible, get creative when things get tight. One vestry member told me, "With our endowment income down, there was talk about cutting our outreach programs. But we didn't want to do that — they're our whole reason for being! So we first asked parishioners to give a '13th month' pledge, to make up the difference. If there still was a difference, we would draw a little more from our endowment than the formula allowed — as a strictly temporary measure."

We believe that parishes of all sizes, small and large, should have endowments.

I've known that parish for years and been impressed by the frequency of their abundance thinking, the regularity with which they review their blessings and strengths and give thanks to God for them. It wasn't a surprise that the parishioners gave almost enough, through the "13th month" extra pledge request, to balance the budget.

Many parishes will cut outreach first without reviewing their options. Remind yourself what is important — i.e., God's work and the mission of your parish. Then review the purpose of your endowment. Does a reduction in the endowment's asset value affect the income? Does a reduction in the income affect the programs? Can the reduction be made up temporarily by more draw down?

By combining clear vision with a sense of abundance about our church's endowment, we can continue our good works and "ride out the storm" of declining market value.

EIGHT

Buildings and Grounds

Heaven is my throne and earth is my footstool. What kind of house will you build for me, says the Lord, or what is my place of rest?
— Acts 7:49

✦ "What about the roof? It's starting to leak again."

✦ "Why didn't anyone tell us the handrail outside was broken? Mrs. Jones broke her wrist the other day when she fell on the ice. Do you think we'll get sued?"

✦ "Speaking of ice, can someone move the shovels from the entryway? And what about those traffic cones inside the door? Do we really have to store them there? We don't have funerals everyday."

✦ "The bushes are blocking the church sign? Well, you can't take them out, even if they are half dead. They're *memorial* bushes!"

For many a vestry, discussions having to do with buildings and grounds issues seem to dominate meetings. And there is a good reason for that, because church properties are sacred space. A daughter may have been married there. A spouse buried in the memorial garden. A child baptized. Through services and luncheons and meetings, hands were held and prayers were said. Connections were made and blessed, and the structure and furnishings of a building helped make that possible.

As Pennsylvania author Sarah Peveler says, we are called to be good stewards of our buildings not because they are our material possessions, *but because they are fundamental tools of our ministry.*

From our parish kitchens, soup springs forth for the homeless. From our sanctuaries, God's word is preached and heard. From our classrooms, children are taught the faith that will sustain them for a lifetime. The work of a vestry is about finding that balance which honors the physical and promotes the spiritual as well.

Keep the Plaster Out of the Soup

Sarah Peveler

Last year, I asked five clergy — evangelical and mainline Protestant, Roman Catholic, Episcopal, and Jewish — to record a short meditation from their own tradition that answered the question, "Why should we spend money on our buildings when there is so much need in the world?"

What could have been a lame joke beginning "there were two ministers, two priests, and a rabbi..." instead resulted in a moving recording in which they tackled the question from Scripture, tradition, and experience. They all agreed that we are called to be good stewards of our buildings, not because they are our material possessions *but because they are fundamental tools of our ministry.*

Confusing landmarks with presence

We Episcopalians do a good job of creating and designating landmarks. Historically, we've had the financial wherewithal to afford the best architects, building materials, and furnishings for our churches. The National Register of Historic Places lists Episcopal churches far out of proportion to our actual presence; the same holds true for state and local registers. Indeed, officials of the New Jersey Trust for Historic Preservation say that, if their preservation grants told the true story of the state's religious character, they'd believe that everyone was either an Episcopalian or Quaker.

According to C. Kirk Hadaway, director of research for the Episcopal Church, parochial reports show that the average age of Episcopal parishes is 106 years. Where does yours fall? Is there a restoration project that would bring joy to your congregation, like the ringing of a bell that has rusted in place?

We have, however, gotten our landmark buildings confused with buildings that mark our presence in community, and therein lies the rub.

Marking place

Our churches mark *place*. From slender colonial spires that once guided ships into eastern ports to the bulky towers of our Gothic cathedrals, our churches dominate the urban landscape. Our forebears wanted to make a statement: "We are here!"

Tiny rural gems like the Bishop Weed churches in Florida and the Bishop Whipple ones in Minnesota catch us by surprise and with delight. Churches are visual anchors in a community whether they dominate the urban streetscape or sit in a grove of trees on a country road, often surrounded by a churchyard.

Our neighbors expect our churches to be there. They pause when the bells ring, they set their watches by the tower clock, and they are our building's guardians when we are not around. Many graffiti artists and burglars have been thwarted in their work by neighbors who "own" the church under siege even if they've never been inside the front doors.

Marking memory

Our churches mark *memory*. Whenever I visit Gethsemane Cathedral in Fargo, I am struck by how this modern building, resembling the grain elevators that break the North Dakota skyline, recalls those fearless Episcopalians who settled the unforgiving prairie. Artifacts from "the cathedral train" (packed with church goods from established congregations on the East Coast) that crossed the state at the turn of the century have been incorporated into Gethsemane's design as have stained-glass windows from the former downtown Fargo cathedral, which was lost to fire. We need these memories to anchor us in our tradition and to link us to those who ministered before and those who will follow.

Marking ministry

Our churches mark *ministry*. Drive down Philadelphia's Germantown Avenue and look up. You will see a sign marking one church's presence in a desperate neighborhood: "We're in Germantown for good."

This bold proclamation celebrates 150 years of service and a successful $2.5 million capital campaign to restore the parish hall that houses an array of social service programs.

When a flood arose, the river burst against that house and could not shake it, because it had been well built.   —Luke 6:48

Our churches open their doors selflessly to the community, and every time one closes or removes deteriorating space from use, day care centers, Scout programs, and 12-Step meetings must find a new home. Partners for Sacred Places' groundbreaking national research on the public value of older and historic religious properties shows that congregations provide an annual average of $140,000 of value to the community through the programs and services they house.

We've gone on the defensive about spending money on our buildings — to restore them or even keep them in good repair. To avoid charges of idolatry, we use our resources to feed the hungry, all the while ignoring the plaster that is falling into the soup pot. As vestry members, we need to rethink our priorities to ensure that our buildings serve our neighbors and us well.

To avoid charges of idolatry, we use our resources to feed the hungry, all the while ignoring the plaster that is falling into the soup pot.

My own parish just finished $3 million dollars of restoration and repair work (as one vestry member put it, a hundred years of deferred maintenance!). We struggle with our operating budget each year; it is an easy call to put off dealing with drainage problems when our programs are growing by leaps and bounds. Or so it seems, until the church school classrooms in the undercroft are flooded yet again.

Worthy of the call

As vestry members, we are the physical stewards of our buildings. They represent one of the greatest assets we have, not only in terms of their financial value but also by what they allow us to do to serve others. Our community knows us by our buildings and how we use them as tools for our ministry. We are called to be good stewards for the present and for the future. Let us be worthy of that call.

Holy Care of Holy Places

ANNABELLE RADCLIFFE-TRENNER

Serving on a buildings and grounds committee is probably one of the most thankless tasks you will ever be asked to do for your church. There is little glamor in maintenance, and most of us live with unrealistically small budgets that result in crisis management care for our churches. Why do we struggle so with maintenance and why is it considered such an inferior responsibility? *If the truth be told, those of us on such committees are indeed the foundation stone, helping to ensure a welcoming shelter to those who arrive at our door.*

For those who seek to find a systematic way to provide good, efficient maintenance, read on. For most congregations, maintenance is unplanned, although there is a direct cost relationship between proactive vs. reactive maintenance. *Planned maintenance can save money.* However, before you can plan, you have to know what you are maintaining. For many of us, this is the first part of the journey to effective planned maintenance.

Begin with a church property register

My recent experience with a dreadful fire at a church in New Jersey has made me aware that parishes first need to know what they own. The Council for the Care of Churches in England provides its churches a property register form; I suggest the same idea for American parishes.

Hats off to Trinity Cathedral in Cleveland and the Diocese of Ohio! Through a major restoration project, the cathedral and diocesan offices are all part of a vibrant center for liturgical, cultural, and artistic events. A new geothermal heating and cooling system undergirds the physical plant, saving an estimated $43,000 a year in heating costs. Italian-style piazzas connect the buildings, reinforcing an open, inviting, restful, and refreshing presence.

Such a register for your parish should include information on the buildings, their documents, and their contents. Much of this information, while it exists, is unorganized and found piecemeal in many of our parishes. An example: the preparation of drawings for a church can cost between $6,000 and $20,000. Most churches have them, but they are often stored in a back room, easily lost to a fire or flood.

Maps, drawings, photographs, deed restrictions, lists of funds and benefactors should be kept in your register. Include as well a list of building contents: furnishings, stained glass, art and sculptures, bells, organs, textiles, books and sheet music.

Use your camera to make this process easier. Vestries also need to understand the historic significance of parish buildings, chronology of construction, building materials, and any deed restrictions.

Condition assessment

Once you have established what you have, you then need to know its condition. Inspection of religious properties is a critical part of putting the planned maintenance puzzle together and helping your parish to be a warm and welcoming space. Why is this step so important?

✠ It saves money.

✠ It allows good fiscal planning and budgeting.

✠ It anticipates major capital expenditures and encourages good building maintenance planning.

Quinquennial (every five years) inspections have been mandated by the Church of England since the 1960s for all churches, and I recommend such a process for American churches as well.

A quinquennial plan takes on the big picture and helps determine the most urgent priorities. Prepared by a professional, the quinquennial report should provide detailed photographic evidence of deteriorated conditions, along with a cost estimate of projected work. The other advantages of a quinquennial is that the work is sensibly phased and results in successful fund-raising.

Scheduled maintenance

You are now ready to move forward with a scheduled maintenance plan. Develop a realistic budget and checklist for each season, including:

✠ Clean gutters and downspouts.

✠ Maintain machinery and equipment on a regularly basis. The best prices for this type of work are before or after the season, e.g., have the furnace serviced in the spring after the heating season.

✠ Repair building materials appropriately. Respect the value of older materials. Remember a one inch piece of wood on an old window frame has approximately twenty growth rings as opposed to four growth rings in a new piece of wood.

✠ Schedule repairs logically. For example, if scaffolding is required to change a light bulb, use the scaffolding to change all the light bulbs at the same time.

✠ Check your plants. When they are close to buildings, especially near sedimentary stones, they become an expensive problem because they encourage biological growth, often resulting in rapid deterioration of the stone mortar.

✠ Test the electrical systems and lightning protection systems every five years.

✤ Develop detailed schedules for cleaning each room and surface. This will help the sexton to plan and budget his cleaning maintenance work.

✤ Include the sexton in meetings because he usually knows more about the buildings than anyone else!

A maintenance manual

Tracking maintenance is best done by keeping a church maintenance manual, and it should be the sole responsibility of one vestry member. A manual should include committee members, an emergency contact list, approved contractors, monthly maintenance schedules, inspection reports, maintenance budgets, long-range plans, meeting minutes, and technical information on repairs.

It is a long road ahead for many of us, but with God's guidance we can pass on to future generations well maintained holy places.

How Does It Work?
Develop an "Owner's Manual"

LEONARD FREEMAN

How do your boilers work? Where do you go to turn on, or down, or whatever, the air conditioners?

The fire alarm has gone off in the middle of the night, and someone from the alarm company is on the phone with you because your church is between clergy, and someone put your name down as the contact "in the meantime." Do you know the alarm code? Is it just a wiring problem caused by the recent electrical outage? Or should the fire department be called?!?!?

Welcome to the world of church maintenance. And that's just for starters.

Most churches, big or small, have systems upon systems devised by nice, well-intentioned, and even skilled people — staff and volunteer — who then moved on, died, or just forgot what they did in the first place.

Whether it's a copy machine blinking at a stumped volunteer or a caterer looking at some piece of parish kitchen equipment saying, "How the heck does *that* work?" someone once knew all the answers, and where to kick the machine. But now it's you . . . and you don't have a clue.

Put it all together

The answer is not brain surgery. It's a parish machinery and maintenance manual, a written record that gets passed down (and a copy or two tucked away somewhere in case someone accidentally walks off with the original). How to do it?

✠ Start where you are with every warranty and instruction manual you can find in the office or in the sexton's closet. Gather them all together and make some copies.

✠ Ask Old Joe and Sally. Get the former sextons and buildings and grounds people in and walk around with them. It's amazing what comes up when you walk into a basement and they say, "Oh, that switch over there? Doesn't work. You push this here, and then turn that."

✠ Ask the building committee about previous construction. Things are often different than what is on the plans. Some things were left off or altered in the actual doing, and somebody knows what and why.

✠ Ask the parish secretaries, current and former. They've probably been asked just about everything by someone along the way and had to figure it out, or who to call. Specific questions can be helpful here. "Where's the XYZ?" or "Why doesn't the dial seem to do anything?"

Don't worry about perfection. Something is better than nothing.

✠ Ask former clergy. On a hot July Saturday it was a rector or vicar the bride's mother was hollering at about the air conditioning. Trust me, they know lots of little stuff — and they know who else to talk to.

✠ Look in the closets. Lurking in them will, no doubt, be lots of things you *don't* need (and should be thrown out, but that's for another day). You just might find plans, ledgers, records, warranties, and more.

✠ *And then, just write it down — whatever you can find.* Don't worry about perfection. Something *is* better than nothing. Alphabetize it by broad and obvious titles so regular folks can hunt through it, and keep it handy, like in the office or sacristy.

And don't forget to throw the new material in as you go forward. Someone someday will be very appreciative.

Local Eternity

Malcolm C. Young

A storm spinning thousands of miles over the Pacific Ocean drives ahead of it warm but powerful southerly winds and dark, foreboding skies. On this late Sunday afternoon most people have already retreated indoors. I can smell wood smoke in the air and damp earth.

I stand at the edge of the lower lawn where newcomers to this church make their first friends during our summer picnics. Some of us dream that the barbecue area on my right will one day be an outdoor labyrinth for walking and praying. Across from here lie the gates to the columbarium where many who led and loved this church are buried.

Two families chose this day to plant three Coast Redwood trees. As I rest on my shovel and our children play in the dirt, it suddenly occurs to me that for many this may be the holiest place on the church campus. The magnitude of what we are doing begins to sink in.

Every observable detail says something about our relationship to each other and to God.

The trees we plant could die from neglect during a hot summer, or they could be alive and exist longer than anything that we do, make, or even touch. Biologists will not consider these trees mature until sometime between A.D. 2500 and 2600.

Some living redwood trees are older than the church. The oldest one lived for twenty-two hundred years. The world's tallest tree at 368 feet is a redwood. As we carry these trees up the hill for the glory of God we come close to eternity.

One could say this about almost every place on the church campus. Every observable detail says something about our relationship to each other and to God. The immaculate chapel sacristy, the cluttered parish hall, the broken floor tiles in the Sunday school classrooms, our street signs (and no skate-boarding signs), the fraying carpet in the sanctuary and expansive grounds all say something about who we are and about our commitment to God.

Whether we intend to or not, our belief in God becomes incarnate in a thousand details that we may not even notice anymore. They say whether we are welcoming or self-satisfied, whether this is a place that people are passionate about right now or one whose glory days are long over. In the most practical sense they show that we care about making God accessible to children and the disabled, or that we are only concerned about people like ourselves.

We do not cease to participate in making God's love known through the objects that surround us.

Last winter a family at our church contributed money to redo the floor and paint the fireside room. With the help of a vestry member, the family also installed a gas fireplace. This cozy place communicates volumes to the families now visiting us in order to learn about our new preschool. I believe that people participating in small groups there are now more likely to experience the love of Christ.

As the storm continues to gather force and the first rain drops fall, we finish planting our redwood trees — but we do not cease to participate in making God's love known through the objects that surround us.

Avoid Unhappy Surprises: Know Your Insurance Policies

STEVE FOLLOS

Editor's note: Making sure that buildings are properly insured often falls under the vestry's care. Acting as an undercover junior warden, I posed some insurance questions to Steve Follos of the Church Insurance Group.

I'm the new warden of St. William's in the Woods. The Deep Woods. I assume that building insurance covers everything, right? Or are there unhappy surprises awaiting me if something goes wrong?

Church property policies come with a deductible that needs to be satisfied with each claim before coverage begins. Most parishes carry a $500 deductible. Larger parishes should consider higher deductibles in return for premium savings.

Property appraisals are an estimate of what an insurance carrier thinks it may cost to replace your damaged or lost property with new materials.

It is possible to be underinsured at time of loss. The risk of being under-insured can be reduced by using a property blanket which combines the totals of all the properties you own.

Insurers appraise the building itself but use a percentage of that value to insure your contents. You should have an inventory stored off premises to make sure all of your personal property is replaced following a loss. *Video inventories are popular because of the speed in which they can be done.* Another option is to have your youth group go to each section of your property and write down anything they see that is not a part of the building.

A visual inventory is a good idea for insurance purposes. Take photos or make a video (or both) of the special items in your church. Use a ruler and good lighting so the actual size of the items is easy to gauge. Identify any fine points or significant features. Update periodically and keep at least one copy off site.

The main exclusion under property insurance is wear and tear. Insurance is different from a warranty. For example, a roof that is a hundred years old and has never been worked on would not be covered if the loss was due solely to its age.

Flood and earthquake damage are also excluded from most policies; coverage can be purchased from your insurer for an additional premium. These coverages typically have a deductible that is a percentage of the building value versus a flat rate deductible. There are typically larger deductibles for hurricanes if you are in a coastal region.

What about the organ? Or that lovely antique picture in the altar guild room?

The organ is considered a part of the building and covered under your building values. It is always a good idea to have your organ appraised to be certain it is included in the building value at the proper limit.

Basic church policies come with a limit on the amount of coverage for fine arts. Parishes should determine if they have adequate limits to cover these valuable items. A vestry should have its parish's fine arts appraised and scheduled on the insurance policy.

Our treasurer's third brother-in-law has a small insurance company. He says that "Allied Mutual Wonderful Insurance" can cover us at 40 percent

Teamwork, Patience, and Humor

Vestry Papers asked wardens from the Consortium of Endowed Parishes their thoughts in planning for long-term maintenance of parish buildings. Teamwork, patience, and humor, they said.

"Every vestry worries about roof leaks and building malfunctions, and it can become obsessed with the buildings the church owns," said Sylvia Temmer of Trinity Church in Princeton, New Jersey. "At the same time, the vestry needs to be aware of the mission of the church, a difficult fence to straddle.

"Involved in a major construction project several years ago, Trinity's vestry commissioned a task force to manage the project, made up of representatives from finance, program, and buildings and grounds committees. Subject to vestry guidance and caps, the task force was able to cut through 'turf issues' and hear all points of view, thus moving the project forward and freeing the vestry."

At St. Andrew's Cathedral in Honolulu, patience is the keyword. "Begun in 1865 the Gothic stone structure here was perceived exempt from maintenance issues," says Duane Leach. "So two years ago we came to grips with reality and achieved a top to bottom evaluation of all aspects of our facility: cathedral, chapel, offices, theater, meeting hall, and two kitchens.

"This is a long project. It will require a funding campaign, continued vision, and great resolve over many years. But then we are the product of over a hundred years of deferred maintenance!"

less than our current coverage. Budgets are tight so that sounds attractive. But how do we know that we won't be making a mistake?

It is always a good idea for a vestry to have insurance company representatives make a presentation before making a change.

There are usually coverage differences that account for premium differences. The vestry may decide that the risk is worth the premium savings but should understand and decide how conservative or aggressive it wants to be in taking on risk. Most parishes would rather pay a little more premium than have the responsibility of paying for a large uncovered claim.

Vestries should ask their insurance agent to look at proposals from other companies and compare the differences in the programs.

Part of our roof blew off, but the insurance adjuster says it's not really his problem and has come in with a settlement that will cover only half of the expected replacement. Is that it? Are we just out of luck?

Most policies are written as replacement cost coverage. This means property is covered for the cost of new materials of like kind or quality. After your deductible, you should receive a check to cover the cost of replacement.

You may have actual cash value coverage. This type of coverage accounts for the depreciation of property. So instead of getting a check to replace the damaged property, you receive a check for what it is worth at time of loss.

If you have replacement costs and are being asked to settle for an amount that is half of what it will cost to have the work done, you should go directly to the carrier who is covering the loss. Support your claim by providing bids for the work that are higher than the offer to settle.

If you still feel you are not receiving a fair settlement, you may seek legal counsel or the help of a public adjuster.

NINE

Conflict and Controversy

We must no longer be children, tossed to and fro and blown about.
...But speaking the truth in love, we must grow up in every way
into him who is the head, into Christ.   —Ephesians 4:15

Vestries are often on the front lines when things get tough — making budget cuts, responding to local disasters, keeping the peace after controversial General Convention decisions, or jumping into the fray if there has been some sort of scandal regarding lay or clergy staff.

It almost doesn't matter if the issue is large or small. Over the years, almost all congregations have experienced parishioners becoming polarized, leaving or threatening to leave, or accusing the clergy and/or vestry of being any number of things: too demanding, too distant, too liberal, too conservative, not caring, dishonest, immoral, or incompetent.

Many congregations handle conflict well. But there are others whose history is so submerged in conflict that its very culture has become one of snarling, backbiting, and gossip. Unfortunately, vestry members can consciously or unconsciously play into the hands of such pressures.

So what is the role of leaders — authentic, Spirit-filled leaders — when it comes to handling conflict and controversy? Remember the common mission, says Georgia author Ward Richards. "When parish leaders embrace conflict and approach it with the recognition that we are called to a common mission as a Christian community, tremendous opportunities arise for spiritual growth and unification."

Mission. Growth. Faith. Trust. Speaking the truth in love. Recognizing that the church has lived with conflict for centuries, but has prevailed. Whatever the conflict or controversy, the vestry must be on the field, ready and informed, speaking the truth in love and, above all, grounded in faith and prayer.

Avoiding the Quick Fix

Peggy Treadwell

The greatest gift vestry members can give their churches is creative, positive challenge and support of their rector(s). Many rectors and churches are done in — particularly in times of uncertainty — by dependent, blaming, reactive parishioners, including vestry members who fail to recognize the importance of their leadership position; they seek quick fixes rather than asking the questions that support their rector's vision and the church's mission. *Never underestimate the power of one true leader, a non-anxious presence in the face of the storm,* especially in these times of high anxiety fueled by terrorism, war, anxious politicians, and the media.

The law of triangles

A new rector accepted the call to a church she later described as "dysfunctional in familiar ways, like my own family." Her inherited senior warden, a fine leader throughout the interim period, began acting like he was the rector, taking over areas where she needed to lead and talking about her to the vestry and administrative staff rather than being direct with her. This paralleled her growing up experience with an alcoholic father, who undermined her abilities and refused to let her grow up.

With coaching, she thought about her issues in both her church and family (the hot spot in one system can be illuminated by the other). I taught her the law of emotional triangles — when two people become uncomfortable with one another, they will use a third person to avoid the risk of direct connection. While this action may seem stabilizing, it in fact keeps the system stuck.

After a month of practice, the rector reported, "Nothing has changed in the situation at my church, but everything has changed because I'm thinking differently about it. I'm detriangling all over the place, asking for direct communication with me rather than through others. I'm going to hang in here for at least four years, keep my vision clear, and rise above the reactivity." That Sunday she preached a brilliant sermon about her dream for the church and vision for the parish.

Vision: seeing systems differently

Vision is a capacity to see the system differently. What does it take to develop this vision and leadership ability in oneself? In *A Failure of Nerve: Leadership in the Age of the Quick Fix,* my mentor, Rabbi Edwin H. Friedman, defines leadership by differentiation as the ability to take maximum responsibility for one's own being and destiny while staying connected with others in the system.

When church leaders — including vestry members by definition — practice thinking and acting on the following four characteristics of leadership by self-differentiation, they tell me, "I now have a direction that makes life and work more interesting and fun!" Jesus' life is our best example of this model of leadership; see biblical references below.

Clarity about one's beliefs

Leaders must develop the ability to pull themselves out of surrounding emotional tensions and think — a challenging task in itself. Recognizing that loneliness and isolation are inherent in their positions, leaders who stay the course often learn to love solitude. *Working at being well-defined oneself takes precedence over trying to understand another.* Practicing clarity on small issues energizes important experience when the larger decisions come along (Mark 1:16–28, 1:35–39, 6:45–52).

Self-definition in relationships

Thoughtful clarity in the way we present our beliefs and ourselves moves people and organizations forward. Non-anxiously saying "I believe, think, perceive . . . " when others are demanding the togetherness position of "we" and being able to take a calm stand in an intense emotional system is a lifelong pursuit. Even so, no one ever achieves 100 percent.

And from the Lutherans: "Welcome to the world of the church, the Body of Christ made up of sinners. Finding conflict in the church should not surprise us. The church is not a perfect place with perfect people. Instead the church is made up of people in need of God's grace and guidance who come and gather in the name of Christ."

—Evangelical Lutheran Church in America, © (ELCA) 2004

Next vestry meeting, experiment with simply containing your reactivity to others (which includes the ability to avoid becoming polarized) by asking yourself, "How can I refrain until I can respond without reacting?" The habit of holy silence can be the best self-definition. What would happen if everyone around the table practiced self-regulation, honoring where one's own self ends and another begins? (Mark 1:40–44; Luke 2:11–52).

Preventing polarization

The poet Rilke once defined love as the capacity of two solitudes to "protect and border and greet each other." That kind of love — knowing where I end and the other begins — is key to preventing polarization, mere gaining of distance, leaving, or cutting off to solve problems.

In my practice of family psychotherapy, I find that cutoffs from others in one's life prevent healing. Further, the tendency to distance and cut off gets passed to the next generation until cutting off becomes the major source of family or parish pathology.

A bishop in one of my groups has begun to take the church genogram (like a family tree covering multi-generations) on his parish visits. He hopes to demonstrate how the processes of cutting off, joining, and self-differentiation are deeply influenced by the way those processes were handled in previous generations, gaining more force as parish life evolved. He illustrates how the capacity of a leader to maintain himself or herself while staying in relationship to God and others is crucial to institutional health and is a balance that one always can improve (Matt. 18:15–20; Mark 2:13–17, 14:22–26).

Self-regulation in the face of sabotage

Leadership by self-differentiation always triggers reactivity. Fearful of change and seeking the comfort of togetherness, people resist new, innovative ideas often when leaders are being most visionary and feel best about their work. In other words, a wise leader can never assume change until he or she has refrained from changing back to the former way of being to calm down the reactivity in the system. *Leadership in uncertain times works best when we take the elongated view, thinking and acting as if we are in this for the long haul.* Most sabotage is mindless, but some is intentional, like the betrayal of Jesus; the moment of truth comes when the leader stays on course. Jesus' ability to "keep on keeping on" despite sabotage led to his resurrection (Mark 14:10–11, 43–51, 16:5–8, 12–20, 10:46–52; Luke 8:43–48).

Skeletons in the Sacristy
LINDSAY HARDIN FREEMAN

Skeletons in the sacristy? We have one — figuratively, at least — in our church. We don't talk about it much; most parishioners haven't even known about it. But like in all family systems, and the church is one, not talking about things isn't always the best option, either.

Our music director says he hears footsteps, or sometimes the laughter of children, behind closed doors late at night. Other staff have heard the same noises when alone in the building. And then, upon comparing stories, we find ourselves thinking: It's Mrs. Camp.

Official vs. nonofficial history

As in most churches, our official history focuses on the positive. In 1888, the local bishop challenged a small group of summer residents of Lake Minnetonka, some twenty miles west of Minneapolis, to bring God into their leisure time by building a church.

Responding to that call was George Camp, a lumber baron, and his wife, Lucy. They built a summer chapel and then donated it to the Diocese of Minnesota as a memorial for their three youngest children, who had died in childhood, and for the impending wedding of their only remaining child, also named Lucy. Written accounts detail the glory of that wedding — what the bride wore, how the church was decorated, etc.

Lingering in the oral history of the parish, however, is this: Mrs. Camp was evidently unable to come to terms with the loss of her three children. Three years after the church was built, she drowned herself across the road in Lake Minnetonka after tying several flatirons around her neck.

While probably not so dramatic, many churches have a range of both joys and tragedies in their past. Most of the happy ones are celebrated, remembered, perhaps embellished. But sad or tragic events may be buried, collectively altered, and pushed aside due to both pain at the time and uncertainty in knowing how to deal with them.

"Most parishes do have stuff in their closets," says Speed Leas of the Alban Institute and a specialist in parish conflict. "Some have worked through it and have had substantial growth. But if you have a place that calls a lot of rectors and just runs through them, or clergy say 'that's a tough place,' then you have a place that needs some attention."

Which begs the question: How do skeletons rumbling around in a church affect current-day life and what do vestries do about them?

"The purpose of looking at the past is not to dwell there, but to see how the past affects the present," says family systems analyst Peggy Treadwell, director of the Counseling Center at St. Columba's Church in Washington, D.C. "There's an old saying, 'anybody can take the truth, but the secrets can kill you?'"

Secrets can kill you

Such secrets, she says, may influence congregational life without parishioners even knowing it. "It's uncanny," she says, "but people will often repeat the same behavior when they don't know the truth. When we know the truth, we have a choice."

Getting at that truth isn't always easy, but the process is essential, adds Bishop Clay Matthews, executive director of the Office of Pastoral Development for the Presiding Bishop. "It makes a tremendous difference, especially with incidents of misconduct, whether they be boundary violations or sexual misconduct or financial misconduct. Should the issues remain in the closet, those are the ones that will come back and affect the health of congregations."

Matthews stresses, however, that the unmasking of skeletons be done carefully, and that getting a trained consultant is helpful. He cautions vestries to be aware of potential litigation, especially if legal agreements have been reached. It may be best to review general developments rather than pinpoint all the details.

At the front door

So, speaking of skeletons, what about Mrs. Camp and the unresolved grief that she so literally laid at our church's front door?

Although her path to the lake was one of inner torture and ultimate isolation, I hope now that she is going from strength to strength in God's kingdom. I believe that she is there with us at the altar rail each Sunday, like so many others. We stand there, none of us perfect, all of us sinners, yet still connected, still one with each other, some visible, others not seen.

And perhaps, through her, God is speaking another message for those of us now at St. Martin's about sharing seemingly unbearable grief. We'll never know. But I pray that we reach out a little more, are more aware of each other's troubles, and are more willing to share our own.

(Additional sources consulted for this article were retired Bishop Claude Payne from the Diocese of Texas and Peggy Herman, a sociologist, professional mediator, and member of St. Gregory's Church in Athens, Georgia.)

Elephants in the Sanctuary

WARD RICHARDS

Conflict. It's inevitable. It occurs every day, in every facet of our lives. And as anyone who has served on a vestry or in any other leadership position in a parish can attest, congregations are not immune.

The word "conflict" often evokes negative images of bickering, power struggles, and infighting. Responding to conflict in unhealthy ways can result in our churches becoming a source of stress and disillusionment rather than solace and peace.

On the other hand, when parish leaders embrace conflict and approach it with the recognition that we are called to a common mission as a Christian community, tremendous opportunities arise for spiritual growth and unification.

Resolving conflict begins with an awareness that people generally respond to it in one or more of the following ways: *Avoidance* — ignoring it in the hope that it will go away; *Force* — making others agree to one's position regardless of the consequences; *Accommodation* — repeatedly giving in to the other person's demands; *Compromise* — both persons giving up certain parts of their respective positions; or *Problem solving* — collaboration and brainstorming options to address the underlying interests of those in conflict.

Trying to completely avoid conflict can often be as harmful as using aggressive means, because wholeness within a community and with God cannot be fully attained by ignoring the elephants in the sanctuary.

If conflict fails to be addressed, resentment and ill will can be created and harbored for many years. Communications conducted in the spirit of love for thy neighbor and speaking the truth in love can result in conflict becoming easier to address and ultimately resolve.

Force, accommodation, and compromise can also be less than desirable in resolving conflict in a parish. Force, for the obvious reasons, and accommodation because the person or group doing all the "giving" usually harbors resentment. Compromise often results in a competitive "give and take" negotiation, frustrating creative brainstorming and potentially bringing resentment.

A win-win solution

Day-to-day experiences, rather than "hot button" issues, are often the cause of conflict in parish life, with new buildings and leadership styles leading the charge. A few years ago, for example, my parish faced conflict resulting from rapid growth. Our building became insufficient to meet our expanding needs. Some thought we should build a parish hall while others wanted a classroom wing. Unable to afford both, we were faced with competing priorities.

> Do not grumble, beloved, against one another, so that you may not be judged; see the Judge is standing at the doors.
>
> —James 5:9

We resolved the conflict, fortunately, through collaborative problem solving. First, the vestry maintained an ongoing dialogue among its members and with others. Several open forums were held providing parishioners the opportunity to discuss the needs of our growing congregation. By including everyone concerned and collectively brainstorming options, a creative win-win solution was found.

The original design for the classroom wing was slightly altered, allowing for a parish hall, complete with a kitchen, to be included as one-third of the new building. The change in design allowed for ease of future conversion of that space into additional classrooms. Enthusiasm for the project increased significantly and the gifts received during the capital campaign exceeded our stated goal.

While the collaborative problem-solving approach certainly worked as a process for resolving conflict in and of itself, *the importance of asking God to be central in our efforts cannot be overstated.* Each meeting began and ended with prayer. Every person involved in leadership was asked to give a personal reflection on what our growing parish meant. By sharing ourselves and by asking the Holy Spirit to be present to lead and guide us, a graceful result was achieved. And through the process, our relationships with each other and with God were greatly enhanced.

Conflict and Controversy: Bringing Wounds and Blessings

Henry Nutt Parsley Jr.

Two of the biggest controversies in the church recently have been the consecration of Bishop Gene Robinson in the Diocese of New Hampshire and the ongoing debate regarding the blessing of same-sex unions. We asked two bishops at General Convention 2003, Henry Nutt Parsley Jr. and Katharine Jefferts Schori, one "nay" and one "yea," to provide their wisdom and insight to vestries struggling with these conflicts.

Conflict can be difficult, especially in the church. The Episcopal Church is presently experiencing a period of disagreement, principally over issues of human sexuality.

While I, as a diocesan bishop, did not favor some of the decisions taken at the last General Convention on these matters, I am steadfastly loyal to the Episcopal Church and believe that with good will and grace we will able to find our way through present disagreements. The conciliar processes of

Anglicanism are often untidy, and discerning the mind of Christ together is always an unfolding reality.

What do leaders do in such times? How do we help our churches manage the stresses of conflict? What helps congregations deal with disagreement in ways that build up rather than weaken our mission?

Wise leadership makes the difference between parishes that have remained unified and focused and those that have become anxious and polarized. I have observed many parishes engaging our present challenges. Let me attempt to distill the wisdom I have seen.

"Do not be anxious," Jesus wisely said in Matthew 6. Centuries later Edwin Friedman observed that unchecked anxiety is one of the most destructive forces in family systems such as the church. Our faith has much to say about managing anxiety through trust in the loving purposes of God. It is well to remember that "Fear not!" is the favorite greeting of the angels in Scripture.

Managing anxiety, so to minimize its impact on the life of the faith community, is a key task of leaders in the church. What Friedman called the "non-anxious presence" of leaders is a crucial gift to the church's life. It is what is needed to help lead the church into "all truth, and in all truth with all peace."

Tolerance and patience

This is especially important in times of conflict. Conflict is endemic to the life of faith, not something to be afraid of. Anglicanism has always recognized that faithful people will have differing points of view on certain theological and social issues. While we share the "faith once delivered to the saints," new issues inevitably arise in the church's experience and the struggle to discern truth is not easy. Anglican comprehensiveness requires both tolerance and patience. A genius of this church has been our capacity to disagree and still worship side by side, steadfast in mission together.

In times of conflict it is essential for leaders to do four things: keep the church focused on its essential mission, communicate well about the issues at hand, respect differing points of view, and trust the Spirit.

First, *staying focused* on mission prevents a parish from becoming centered on anything other than Christ and his work. In parishes where leaders become fixated on issues — whether disagreements over chancel furniture, new hymnody, or human sexuality — the parish suffers. As Casey Stengel once said, "The main thing is to make the main thing the main thing." As issues come and go, healthy people expect the church to keep its focus on worship, teaching and pastoral care, and reaching out to love and serve others. The vestry is called to be a focus of unity, where mission is central and issues are addressed but not allowed to dominate.

From an informed poll of our readers:

What do laity look to clergy for in times of crisis? Our most frequent and impassioned answer: Spiritual guidance in understanding the forces of evil and why bad things happen — and how to best respond. Other answers:

1. Be there — in the pulpit, by the hospital bed, in the home.
2. Be pastoral — pray, bless, forgive.
3. Be steady — like a sturdy tree, flexible but strong.
4. Be creative — especially with parish conflicts.
5. Give reassurance — show the light of Christ.
6. Share hope.

What do clergy look to laity for in times of crisis?

1. Pray — for the situation and for the clergy.
2. Be supportive — of those grieving and the clergy.
3. Be present — show up. No gesture is too small.
4. Do not gossip.
5. Maintain confidences — yours is a key role and discretion must be used.
6. Be clear and ready to focus — come prepared to gently lead.

Secondly, *good communication minimizes anxiety* that people feel when they do not know what is going on. Healthy churches deal with issues openly rather than hide from them. In our current conflict it helps to explain the church's teaching on sexual ethics and the questions being raised regarding pastoral and moral guidance for persons in the church who are homosexually oriented, as we are coming to understand this reality.

As a bishop I care deeply about the church's inclusion and pastoral care for all persons and for justice. Yet I do not believe that we have found an adequate new *consensus fidelium* about same-sex relationships. It has been helpful for me to explain my conscientious decision not to consent to the election of Bishop Robinson and my steadfast conviction about being loyal to the church as we struggle through these matters. Reasonable people can disagree, but we all need to understand what the issues are and how the church is facing them.

Third, *leaders must listen* to the range of opinions always present in a congregation. Otherwise polarization quickly results. When persons feel that they are being heard and different views respected, anxiety is diminished and trust is enhanced. When the leaders of a church listen to only one point of view, the community becomes divided. Our tradition is always best at "both/and" thinking rather than "either/or" thinking.

Finally, in times of conflict, *leaders say their prayers* and help congregations trust Jesus' promise that the Spirit will guide us into all truth. Our faith holds that God is at work in all things. Even disagreement can be a channel for God to shape and form us in his service. Leaders keep their attention on God and trust that, as George Herbert wrote, "God moves in mysterious ways his wonders to perform." This is our spiritual foundation.

It is painful when faithful people disagree and at times hurt each other. Through it, nonetheless, we can grow in faith and commitment. Like Jacob wrestling with the angel, through conflict we are both wounded and blessed. Leaders are called to love the church through such difficult times and trust God for the rest.

God Is Still at Work: When Conflict and Hope Abound

KATHARINE JEFFERTS SCHORI

Conflict and controversy are intrinsic to the church, even if many of us would prefer to live and worship in communities that never disagreed about anything. Jesus himself was executed in response to the controversy he stirred up; and the church has not been without conflict since. Even though we may heatedly disagree, we do aspire to respond to differences without resorting to crucifixion!

For us as leaders, the task of managing conflict is ever-present. A leader becomes and remains a leader by virtue of being able to make a clear decision and encouraging others to respond to that decision. Christians do that every day in responding to the expectations of the baptismal covenant, and Christians become leaders in their daily ministry as they experience and foster transformation in themselves and the world around them.

Conflict at its most basic is a difference between one or more views of the way things are or should be. In theological terms, we are in conflict because we have not yet arrived at the fullness of the Kingdom of God, and we will be in conflict until the Second Coming. Simply put, that means that God is still at work, and, therefore, hope should abound! Conflict is a sign of life and a necessary precursor to growth.

That said, conflict still generates fear or discomfort in most of us.

Leaders manage their reactions

Effective leaders learn to manage their own emotional reactions to conflict in ways that allow others to respond more rationally and less emotionally. The less anxious a leader is about the conflict, the more able others will be to engage the conflict constructively. Jesus' public ministry gives repeated examples of this principle of leadership.

The most public conflict in the Episcopal Church and Anglican Communion right now has to do with the controversial decisions of the 74th General Convention about matters of human sexuality. That particular conflict is being played out in a variety of ways around the church and the Communion, and it is a more painful issue in some places than others.

I did vote to consent to the election of the Reverend V. Gene Robinson as bishop of New Hampshire, and I also voted to pass Resolution CO51, which recognized that blessing same-sex unions is within the bounds of our common life as Episcopalians. Those decisions were far less controversial in Nevada than they were in some places, but they still engendered a fair bit of heat. The real struggle in Nevada came at our diocesan convention in 2003, when the Integrity chapter presented a resolution asking for a policy on same-sex blessings.

Suddenly the issue was not across the country; it was here in people's own worship communities. The convention eventually agreed to continue (and in many cases, begin) conversation about matters of human sexuality in their own congregations and regional gatherings, and to permit, with the bishop's consent, congregations to develop their own policies. The conversations in the year following showed a remarkable growth in community. Most were marked by far more light than heat, especially when individuals were willing to ask hard questions and share their own confusion and vulnerability.

The ability of a few leaders to model appropriate self-disclosure and respectful questioning made an enormous difference. The hard work of those conversations did not lead to uniformity of opinion by any means, but it did demonstrate to all who took part that their opinions were valued. The few who left the Episcopal Church were generally not those who took part in those discussions, and the congregations who avoided dealing with these issues have missed the true vitality that comes from wrestling with God.

Holding decisions lightly

The most helpful aspect of leadership in a conflict is the ability to be clear about the decision that has been made without being defensive or argumentative. At the same time, a good leader is able to hold that decision lightly, with enough humility to recognize that no one individual ever holds the fullness of Truth in him or herself. We rarely make highly significant decisions that cannot later be revisited if better information comes to light. If we believe that God is present with us, and the Spirit still at work, then sometimes our decisions will change.

Our own church is a wonderful example, in its historic ability to hold differing positions in tension — Catholic and Reformed, high and low styles of worship, music that spans a millennium, and social policy that incenses some and gladdens the hearts of others.

Our ability to provide leadership in communities experiencing conflict is also a gift to the wider world. Churches are laboratories for daily labor; they are gymnasia where we train for life as Christians in the world. The Reign of God requires the ministry of each one of us, whether or not we can agree on exactly what it will look like!

TEN

Leadership in Times of Crisis

And a great storm of wind arose, and the waves beat into the boat, so that the boat was already filling.... They woke him and said to him, "Teacher, do you not care if we perish?" And he awoke and rebuked the wind, and said to the sea, "Peace! Be still!"... And the wind ceased. He said to them, "Why are you afraid? Have you no faith?" —Mark 4:37–40

Conflict in congregational life is like snow in Minnesota: it's going to happen. But if the conflict grows too large, or if disaster strikes too harshly, parishes will shift into crisis management. And then one of two things will happen. A congregation will reach down into its roots, springing forth with new life and new growth — or the group will wither and die.

Our writers in this chapter talk about the steps preceding such developments, for, as they argue, there is often time before such an event occurs where healing needs to take place.

Alban Institute founder Loren Mead says three elements are critical: working as a vestry/clergy team; keeping your eye on what members of the congregation really care about; and maintaining some perspective.

"Christians have several stories of boats in turbulent waters," Mead suggests, "and we ought to remember who is really in charge. Not us. We do the best we can. We lean to the oars. We try to keep our nerve. The final outcome is not up to us."

The final outcome is not up to us, but many of the preceding steps are. With God's grace and our faith in the ultimate leadership of the boat, we are indeed free to live the life of perfect service in Christ.

Fit to Go the Distance

William G. Andersen Jr.

Don't read this piece if you are looking for some McGod off the shelf, for religious leadership in uncertain times is not about a quick fix. Call a consultant or read one of the thousands of books with "leadership" in the title for that kind of help.

A response to clergy and lay leaders about leadership in uncertain times is a two-handed answer: on the one hand, it is easy; on the other, it is hard. It is easy because what you need is already at hand. It is hard because it may take another way of looking at things to know how to uncover and use them.

One of the most valued things I learned from a former rector/mentor was how to apply practical theology to parish decision making. And that drawing forth of theological conviction makes us who we are as Christians. We consciously or unconsciously draw on our Christian heritage, our journey experience, and how, at the moment, we hear God's call.

What does that mean for leadership in uncertain times? Certainly, on a macro scale, what has happened in the church post–General Convention has added a measure of uncertainty or unease to the church's life. But at the congregational level, we experience uncertainty at different times as well — for example, when there is a significant shift in leadership during a transition, or when the congregation is conflicted over a challenging issue. (In that regard a Duke study, "Pulpit and Pew," found that the top three causes of conflict in congregational life did not include issues of sexuality, but rather, leadership style, program emphasis, and finances.)

Health, wholeness, and holiness

So in an uncertain time, whether an unsettling churchwide issue, a poor economy that generates scarcity thinking, or program conflict, what is a vestry leader or warden to do? A foundational start is to remember that what we seek for clergy and congregational life is health, wholeness, and holiness. Years of research, fact finding, and practice by the Foundation have proved the need for those qualities to sustain congregational vitality.

How, then, do we emulate those qualities in our leadership — how are we healthy, whole, and holy leaders? Jim Fenhagen, in his book *Invitation to Holiness*, gives us a clue about what it means to be that kind of religious leader. "Wholeness," he says, is to be " ... in tune with the spirit of God who moves within me." Wholeness is the "seedbed for holiness." Holiness is leaning toward God.

Jim adds, "It is the way we perceive reality and the way we act on those perceptions." I call it our sense of "Godness." He adds that "conversion and transformation" are also ingredients in the mix. For those like me who are feeling a bit intimidated by that job description, think about the definition of the church "as a group of people who are slowly getting the idea." It fits.

Let me use as an example what the Foundation heard in the aftermath of General Convention's "consent" decision. As we compiled all the reports from our contacts, it was clear that the majority of people in congregations did not have an ideological stance about the decision. What they were feeling was bewilderment about the momentousness of the decision's impact. Many felt that "it crept up on us" without warning and without a plan for dealing with how to understand it. *How did this happen? What does it mean? Who will help us figure it out?*

Be proactive, neutral, and non-anxious

In a situation where there is unease, or tension is building, it is time to quietly work at your information gathering activities. Be proactive, neutral, and a non-anxious presence. And remember that as chief listeners, you are not required to be the chief-on-the-spot fixers! Rather, it is time to mine coffee hours and other occasions to hear what people are saying and feeling. Instead of declarative statements about the topic-du-jour, it's time for the "I wonder" questions. During times of stress, more intentional listening is in order.

We are beginning to see as we never saw before that we are truly in the world and yet ultimately not of it. For we are groping to the realization that above all else, we are called to be saints.
— Seminary student Jonathan Daniels shortly before he was killed while protecting a young African American girl, Selma, Alabama, 1965

My colleague warden and I used to conduct "fireside chats" when needed. We simply announced that the wardens would be available at a certain time at the church and invited anyone with particular concerns to come and talk. (The only time we were slightly overwhelmed was when the sale of the rectory was being considered; it was more like a public hearing than a quiet conversation!)

Once the pulse taking is concluded, the next step involves discernment about an appropriate response to the community. It is time for the vestry to be a self-energized, collective, theological resource, asking: How does Scripture guide us? What prayer supports us? How does quiet time allow the spirit to speak? And remember the importance of pausing to ask, "What are we learning?" Some recording of events for future reference will be helpful.

Religious leadership is different

This simple repeated cycle of Scripture, prayer, and quiet time during a meeting will provide the leads to a healthy, whole, and holy outcome. After all, it is what distinguishes us as religious leaders from corporate or civic leaders.

And, above all, we shouldn't forget the scriptural mandate we all bear to build up the Body of Christ. For in the midst of stressful times, it is easy to choose sides and look for winners and losers, and that usually is not helpful. Because, in the end, building up the Body is a Spirit-led, collegial activity — God, people, and priest engaged with each other.

Wisdom Gathered, Lessons Learned

LOREN MEAD

There *are* crises that come along that you have to meet. Most of us fumble our way through and manage not to sink the boat while we're doing it. Trust that in most cases, even the most terrible crisis will look different in a month and may be forgotten in a year. Take a deep breath. Do the best you can. Here are suggestions of things I've found helpful:

✚ **Work as a vestry/clergy team on building the team.** Work on simple skills — how to treat each other decently in the middle of tensions; how to listen to what other people are saying — both their words and the emotions behind the words. Avoid getting impatient and pushing for decisions before others are comfortable with what's up. Look out for "ganging up" by one "side" of an argument against the others. Be sure you have clear rules about how you make decisions. Make sure that committees and working groups include people who don't agree with each other. Don't let somebody's panic infect the whole vestry. Don't let the loud voices push actions or decisions prematurely.

✚ **Keep your eye on what members of the congregation really care about.** Keep the roof on the place. Be sure the pastor is freed up to do the pastoring people need, seeing that visitors are received hospitably, and looking out for people whom society neglects (the poor and homeless).

✛ **Work on keeping some perspective**:

- Get to church regularly and pitch in to the worship. Sing your lungs out. I find that when I'm most tense it helps to get to an extra Eucharist (early morning, sometimes in another parish is what works best for me).
- Do some reading that gets behind the uncertainty of the times.

Christians have several stories of boats in turbulent waters, and we ought to remember who is really in charge.

- Look out for "the common wisdom" or "what everybody wants us to do." Although those words can seem compelling, it is remarkable how often they are wrong. In dealing with a big issue (war and peace, sexuality, abortion) we often do the very thing we've found out works least well — gather up proponents of the different points of view and launch a debate. Almost always that strategy, which seems so simple and useful, only exacerbates the issue and makes people madder at each other. There are ways to work at those controversial issues while building our sense of community with each other. Debates don't do that.
- Remember that the work of the vestry/clergy team is to build ministry. Not to fix everything. Not to determine who or what is "right." Uncertain times by definition are uncertain. No amount of shouting at one another will reduce the uncertainty. Indeed, if you are in a boat in turbulent seas it doesn't help to jump up and down or try to throw some folks overboard. That's likely to capsize the boat, not fix the problem.

The turbulence of the seas comes from the wind, not from how the people in the boat are acting. Christians have several stories of boats in turbulent waters, and we ought to remember who is really in charge. Not us. We do the best we can. We lean to the oars. We try to keep our nerve. The final outcome is not up to us. Our job is to hold steady and to use this challenge to become a stronger, steadier team for the *next* storm, which is surely just beyond the horizon.

Flames and Faith

Judy Hoover

The phone rang at 4:35 a.m. on Sunday morning. "Is this the Reverend Judy Hoover?" I responded affirmatively although I was trying to clear my brain. "This is the Hennepin County dispatcher. Can you respond to an emergency?" I am a volunteer chaplain and sometimes on call to assist the Police when there is an emergency.

I tried to justify not responding because it had been only eight days since my husband of forty-seven years had died, and I was exhausted physically and emotionally. I suggested another chaplain, but she went on. "Who would you like me to call? Your church is fully engulfed in fire!" I called the senior warden while hurrying to the church. Within less than an hour, at least half the membership was there, watching helplessly as the thirty-five-year-old church burned to the ground.

Reporters from five TV stations came immediately to the five-alarm blaze. One parishioner thought to bring the church directory, and those with cell phones made key phone calls. Our congressman, Jim Ramstad, came to stand with us. The Salvation Army brought blankets, food, and coffee.

We wept together and reminisced. We laughed about the things we always wanted to change and we spoke of rebuilding as soon as possible. The convener from a nearby church called and offered their building for a service later in the day.

Some tips

So what have we learned since then? A multitude of lessons, too numerous for this page. Here are a few:

✚ God is with us and will be our strength and our salvation, no matter what happens.

✚ Get the area cordoned off as soon as possible, as it is a major liability risk.

✚ Call your insurance company ASAP for emergency funds and an adjuster to begin the process of evaluating the loss.

✚ After a disaster like this, there is a sense of loss of control and a power vacuum in the congregation. All those who have always wanted to change something come forward to assert themselves. Occasionally there are potentially divisive disagreements over things that do not warrant the attention or emotion that is evoked. This is what happens when the entire congregation is suffering from grief and loss all at the same time.

+ Immediately put parishioners to work making lists of all the contents of the building. A better idea is to have them do it *now* when there is no loss. Take pictures or video shots of the church inside and outside.

+ Anyone in the congregation who has personal property on the premises must have a record of what it is and its value. (We had a Steinway on loan. Fortunately, I had asked the owner to cover it with her own insurance, as it would not have been insured under our policy.)

+ Clergy should have a listing of personally owned vestments and their books. These should be specially listed in their homeowners' policy or they will not be covered as they are considered "business or professional" properties. (Bad news for me, as I lost about $10,000 worth of books.)

+ Gather the congregation together soon to talk about its loss and what it wants to preserve.

+ Make arrangements for grief counseling for those who are in pain. Children and youth should be included in some form of recognition of their sense of loss. (Many of our acolytes were devastated by losing their crosses.)

+ Many people step forward to offer help and contributions. Everything from old family organs to free services may be offered. Be sure what is offered is something you really need or want.

+ Store insurance coverage away from the church; duplicate it and put it in two places, one a safety deposit box.

+ Back up or duplicate financial and parish records and store them off campus. We had our financials off site, but the parish records were not.

+ Set up a system for thanking people for their prayers, contributions, and concern. (One parishioner has sent over 150 thank you notes on our behalf. I have sent over 300 that were memorials for my husband.) It is a big task.

There are many more learnings but this is what occurs to me right now. I just keep reminding myself that all things work together for those who love God and keep moving forward.

When the Waves Are High

Dick Kurth

I have been privileged to enjoy a number of explicit leadership roles in my life. People who have a real stake in the outcome have deliberately given me authority and trusted me to use that authority well on their behalf.

The leadership role of a vestry is to remember accurately where the church community has been, to shed light on where it is now, and to discern where it needs to go and how it might get there. There must be a shared notion, regularly tested and never too precise or final, of where the far shore is. Your job as a leader of the vestry is to pilot the boat toward that often dim shore.

Accepting our vulnerability and our inability to control people and events is the ground for leadership.

But what about crisis leadership? Now the waves are high, the boat is full of water, and the shore is not visible at all. The anguished cry is "Who will lead us?"

We might find the leadership in people from whom we explicitly expect it. Then again, we might not. Where to turn, whom to follow?

We are all familiar with how an unexpected situation can produce leaders we didn't know we had. So, how will we recognize the leaders at such a time? More importantly, how will they recognize themselves?

Leaders are those who can see a situation clearly and act accordingly because they know who they are.

What is it that leaders must know about themselves? That all of us — individually, in small groups, and in community — are vulnerable. Accepting our vulnerability and our inability to control people and events is the ground for leadership. We can shape, we can set direction and be intentional, but we can't control. Aligning our behavior to this knowledge is deeply countercultural, but isn't going against the grain a special gift of the church?

In a crisis, the first question is not "what happened?" but "who am I?" Second, "who are we?" Only with answers to the question of who you are can you respond to events instead of react to them.

Hearing the call to leadership

Leadership responds; it does not react. We are called to move forward, not to defend. To respond to a call you must first hear the call.

Response has to do with seeing, noticing, paying attention to what is right in front of you. Being there, fully present at all times. It does not have to do with solving problems (reacting). It does not have to do with knowing the answers. In fact, it is crucial not to give answers when there are none, and this too is countercultural; to act as if you have the answers when you do not prolongs a crisis by increasing anxiety. It is a common abuse of the authority and trust that has been invested in you.

The waves have risen and the surging sea is dangerous, but we do not fear drowning for we stand upon the rock. Let the sea surge! It cannot destroy the rock. Let the waves rise! They cannot sink the boat of Jesus.

—John Chrysostom, bishop of Constantinople, from the homily preached in AD 409 before he was sent into exile by the Romans, where he died from exhaustion and starvation.

Response means showing your love. You have to see around corners and through walls and hear even the smallest insistent sound. This cannot be done if you think you know the answers, if you are certain that you know where the shore is before anybody else does. You cannot see clearly through the cataracts of your own opinions and you cannot hear well through the din of your own problem-solving inner voice, either.

Showing love means caring for the human being first, attending to her, listening to him, banishing anxiety. Such love will help you lead people to the far shore.

We saw this leadership quality abundantly in Rudy Giuliani from the very first hours of the World Trade Center attack. He was everywhere present, tireless, attending to people, telling them what he knew, being honest when he didn't know, not hiding his grief, and throughout it reminding us that as New Yorkers we would get through this (as in our deepest hearts we already knew we would, since as humans we have to get through it). His love and attention to this city laid a strong foundation for the future.

Telling the truth

When I was six and my brother was five, we moved to England. As we flew from Los Angeles to London across the North Pole (this was 1958), he asked me if the plane would crash. I said it might and it might not. That was of course the truth. I believe in telling the truth. After being bothered by my answer for forty-three years, he recently said to me, "All I wanted was for you to say, 'Everything will be all right.' That's all." That would have been the truth too, even if we had crashed.

Seeing what people need and helping them to get it while telling the truth is what leadership is all about. In crisis or not, that is the heart of my faith journey.

Vestries: Catalysts for Healing
TITUS PRESLER

"What do you think is going to happen?" is a question I hear often in discussions of the aftermath of the sexuality decisions of the 2003 General Convention. "I don't know," is the most frequent and the most honest answer. So this is an uncertain time.

All times are uncertain in that we cannot know the future. Strategic planning in congregations, though, is based on a discernment of what's happening in the town or city, what trajectories are developing, and how God might be calling the congregation to respond in mission.

Conflict within the church is what makes this time especially uncertain. The sexuality issue has provoked conflicts in congregations, dioceses, the Episcopal Church as a whole, and the Anglican Communion. This conflict blurs the identity of the "we" when you want to say, "We are called to participate in God's mission in the world." A congregation might have been planning an innovative outreach, but conflicted feelings about the Episcopal Church's direction have sapped the commitment of key people in the initiative.

Conflict evokes fear. We fear being hurt and hurting others. We fear encounters becoming volatile. We fear taking initiative and then being left out on a limb. Ultimately, fear undermines our commitment to engaging with one another. Fear produces isolation.

Reducing fear, building trust
What is the role of vestry members in the uncertainty of this conflicted time?

A leader is a person whose presence and vision catalyze commitment and action in others. In personal presence, the leader stays engaged and makes a special effort to avoid isolation. In fearful times especially, leaders need to be conveners, gathering people specifically to talk with one another across the divides of theological differences.

In this convening role, vestry members can take their cue from the church's bishops, who in the half-year since convention, have spent much time and energy gathering the people of their dioceses for conversation with one another. This ministry has been crucial in helping the church hold together as well as it has. Many congregations have undertaken similar conversations, and it is important that vestries and clergy continue that practice as events continue to unfold. Wisely guided, conversation reduces fear, builds trust, and restores community.

Staying the mission course

In vision, the leader stays the mission course. In the midst of fear and turmoil, the leader stays deeply and passionately engaged in the mission to which God is calling the community. Seekers off the street and church members alike want to be part of communities that are doing God's work beyond themselves — "out there in the world" — and they get discouraged when a congregation's energies are preoccupied with internal conflicts.

> *For he shall give his angels charge over you,*
> *to keep you in all your ways.*
> *They shall bear you in their hands,*
> *lest you dash your foot against a stone.*
> —Psalm 91:11–12

At the same time, vestry members need to embrace mission through the current conflict, not instead of the current conflict. People on all sides of this conflict have important mission concerns in the conflict. In fact, mission concern is what makes people as passionate as they are about their views. So this is a good time to return to your parish's mission statement. Talk as a vestry and as a congregation about how your mission relates to the conflict and how you can engage God's mission through the dynamics of the conflict.

The long view

In presence and vision, leaders take the long view and the wide view. Taking the long view means realizing that the course of the church's current conflict will take some time. No one can say how long, but certainly years, not months. Realize that, like your diocese and the general church, your congregation's evolution over this conflict will be long term. So pace yourself. Avoid expending all your patience and energy over a few months. Plan to stay with the issue for several months, at least. Be creative about how the congregation moves forward with the issue in spirituality, community life, education, and mission outreach.

Taking the wide view right now means staying in touch with and learning from Episcopal and Anglican companions in other places. If people in your congregation are generally of one mind, work with your rector and vestry members and talk with the clergy and vestry of a differently minded congregation nearby. Take the opportunity to talk with visitors from other parts of the country.

Visitors from other parts of the Anglican Communion are especially helpful to engage, whether they're from Nigeria or Nicaragua, Canada or Cameroun. Recently a bishop from Malawi observed to me, "Colonialism had the effect of broadening our horizons, so that we in Africa had to think globally." Ironically, we within what is currently the sole global superpower can often be quite local in our perspective, and that applies to our church thinking as well as our geopolitics.

Missionaries from your diocese to other parts of the world can help you gain access to viewpoints around the communion, both from their own experience and through connecting you with fellow Anglicans. Trolling the Internet can help you make connections and sample other perspectives.

Such presence and vision in you as a vestry member will catalyze commitment and action in your congregation. The Catechism says our mission is to "restore all people to unity with God and each another in Christ." That's reconciliation. That's what God is up to in the world. That's your leadership task in this moment.

O Lord, support us all the day long, until the shadows lengthen, and the evening comes, and the busy world is hushed, and the fever of life is over, and our work is done. Then in thy mercy, grant us a safe lodging, and a holy rest, and peace at the last. Amen.

— The Book of Common Prayer, page 833